The Restaurant TABLE TURNOVER PLAYBOOK

Discover the Secret to Explosive Growth by Avoiding These 5 Mistakes

DONOVAN GARETT

Copyright © 2024 AlgoRhythms Studios, Ltd.

All rights reserved.

Any attempt to reproduce, translate and/or distribute in any medium any part of this work beyond that permitted by Section 107 or 108 of the 1976 United States Copyright Act without express written consent by the copyright owner is illegal. No part of this publication may be duplicated, stored in a retrieval system, or transmitted in any form or by any means electronic, mechanical, photocopied, recorded or otherwise, without the prior written permission of the publisher. Requests for permission or further information can be sent by U.S. mail at the following address:

AlgoRhythms Studios, Ltd.

P.O. BOX 35643

Cleveland, Ohio 44135

United States of America

DISCLAIMER. This publication is intended (but not guaranteed) to provide accurate information in regard to the subject matter covered. Some information may not be applicable to every reader or every situation. It is sold with the understanding that neither the author, publisher nor any other person or entity connected with the creation, publication or distribution of this publication provides legal, accounting, real estate or other professional services. If expert assistance is required, the services of a competent professional should be sought. Furthermore, this publication may contain business strategies, marketing methods, and other statements that, regardless of the experiences of some, may not produce the same results for you. The author, publisher, and all parties engaged in the creation and distribution of this publication make absolutely no guarantee, expressed or implied, that by following the statements in this publication you will make any money or improve current profits, as there are several factors and variables that come into play regarding any given business. Results will depend on your business model, the conditions of the marketplace, the experience of the individual, and situations and elements that are beyond your control. As with any business endeavor, you assume all risk related to investment and money based on your own discretion and at your own potential expense.

PRINT ISBN: 978-1-963267-00-6

E-BOOK ISBN: 978-1-963267-01-3

Printed in the United States of America

Contents

SECTION 1   1
    Welcome

1. Introduction   3
    Why I'm So Passionate
    Restaurants are More Than Places to Eat
    Table Turnover in a Post-Pandemic World
    An Overview of What's In the Book

2. Patent vs. Latent Mistakes: Unmasking the Unseen   11
    Patent Mistakes: The Obvious Blunders
    Latent Mistakes: The Silent Success Killers
    The "Golden Blindfold": When Apparent Success Masks Critical Mistakes

3. Seeing the Bigger Picture: From Situational Blindness to Operational Clarity   27
    Situational Blindness in Small Restaurants
    Growth Pains & Scaling Challenges
    Why Growing & Scaling
    Can Feel Overwhelming

SECTION 2   45
The 5 Table Turnover Mistakes

4. Mistake #1: Poor Reservation Management   47
   Consequences of
   Poor Reservation Management
   Reservation Management Best Practices
   Key Takeaways

5. Mistake #2: Slow Service and Kitchen Delays   69
   Impact on Customer Wait Times
   Service Efficiency Best Practices
   Key Takeaways

6. Mistake #3: Poor Seating Optimization   89
   Why Seating Optimization is Critical
   Seating Optimization Strategies
   Key Takeaways

7. Mistake #4: Poor Waitlist Management   111
   Understanding Waitlist Management
   Consequences of
   Poor Waitlist Management
   Waitlist Management Best Practices
   Key Takeaways

8. Mistake #5: Poor Menu Presentation   133
   What is Poor Menu Presentation?
   Consequences of Poor Menu Presentation
   Menu Presentation Best Practices
   Key Takeaways

SECTION 3   165
   Staff Training, Technology, Social Media & Reputation Management

9. Staff Training and Customer Service   167
   The Importance of Staff Training
   Creating a Positive Workplace Culture
   Staff's Impact on Table Turnover
   Staff's Impact on Profitability
   Continuous Training and Development
   Key Takeaways

10. Embracing Technology for Long-Term Success   191
   The Role of Technology in Restaurant Operations
   Key Takeaways

11. Implementing Technology Solutions in Your Restaurant   205
   Assessing Your Restaurant's Needs
   Point-of-Sale (POS) Systems
   QR Codes and Virtual Menus
   3rd Party Reservation Systems
   Delivery Platform Integration
   Key Takeaways

12. Social Media, Reputation Management, and Data Security   235
   Social Media and Online Reviews
   Data Security and Compliance
   Key Takeaways

SECTION 4   251
Wrap-Up and Contact Information

13. Final Thoughts and Contact Information   253
    Stay in Touch

Also By Donovan Garett   255

SECTION 1

Welcome

In this section, we'll set the stage for our journey together. I'll share why I'm so passionate about the profitability of small, local, independent restaurants. Then, we'll lay the foundation for our discussion of the five most common table turnover mistakes that could prevent your restaurant from realizing its true potential.

Before tackling the 5 table turnover mistakes, though, we'll first discuss the fundamental differences between patent and latent mistakes, then take a deep dive into situational awareness (or lack thereof), which is an aggravating factor for why table turnover mistakes often persist for so long.

I'm thrilled to be on this journey with you.

Let's begin.

CHAPTER 1
Introduction

"Success is a journey, not a destination. The doing is often more important than the outcome."

Arthur Ashe

FIRST AND FOREMOST, thank you for taking a chance and buying this book. It has taken many early mornings, late nights, sticky notes, interviews, advice from friends and colleagues, and plenty of sips of bourbon to get here.

I'll start off with a confession. Putting together a book like this can be quite a challenge. Not only are there many different types of restaurant operating models, but the pace of change influencing the restaurant industry today is truly staggering.

If you have read any of my other books (thank you), you may have noticed that they focused on showing how to get diners into your restaurant through marketing, advertising, social media, etc., and on keeping them via well-crafted loyalty programs. However, in this book, we'll shift the focus a bit and discuss what to do with them once they arrive.

Why I'm So Passionate

At this point, you might be wondering why I'm so passionate about small, local, independent restaurants. Well, the answer is both simple and complex. So, I'll start with the simple answer.

As is often the case throughout history, new challenges and opportunities require new thinking, strategies, and tactics. The COVID-19 pandemic has required all businesses (including your restaurant) to fundamentally rethink how they operate.

Most notably, the way that restaurants reach and engage with customers has been irreversibly altered. The *"good old days"* of simply hanging out an "open" sign and expecting word-of-mouth to do all of your advertising for you are long gone.

Why?

Because people no longer aimlessly wander around the neighborhood as they once did. As a result, there is a strong chance that you may open your doors and hardly anyone even knows your restaurant exists – that is, if you don't invest in marketing.

Today's consumers are much different from those of past decades. They are distracted by the world around them. So, since they aren't actively looking for your restaurant, **you** must put forth the effort to find **them**.

You must be on the internet, apps, and platforms that they frequent. They demand convenience and are rarely willing to wait more than a few minutes for anything. Small restaurant owners who fail to realize this miss valuable opportunities to reach, attract, engage, and retain customers.

My professional career began over 30 years ago with a keen interest in hospitality, foodservice, and restaurant operations. However, a series of serendipitous events led me into technology, software engineering, web design, and strategic marketing.

Today, as the owner of a web design and restaurant marketing agency, I am on a mission to support small independent restaurant owners who lack guidance and know how to navigate the challenges that the post-pandemic economy has introduced.

Okay, well, that was the simple answer.

Here's the more complex answer.

Restaurants are More Than Places to Eat

As we get older, there are many things that we simply don't remember anymore. However, a good meal at a restaurant with people we care about is not one of them. Good meals shared with friends and family are some of our fondest memories, whether at home, on vacation, or during a special occasion.

In fact, McDonald's has been counting on this strategy for decades.

How so?

Well, thinking back as a kid, who can forget the rush of excitement when the car suddenly turned into the McDonald's drive-thru? The eager anticipation of a Happy Meal always seemed to brighten the day, no matter what was going on in life.

Because all of those positive childhood memories are deeply ingrained in the subconscious minds of McDonalds' customers, they instill a sense of fondness for the brand. Over time, this fondness turns to staunch loyalty. Once instilled, loyalty simply needs a trigger to activate buying behavior.

What's the trigger?

It could be a commercial during your favorite TV show, a billboard, or a marketing campaign. Years, even decades, later – these fond childhood memories can be instantly brought to the forefront of our conscious minds with advertising. This is one of the many genius strategies that has helped McDonald's gain monumental success for generations.

In a larger sense, restaurants represent much more than just a place to eat. They offer unique opportunities to sample cuisine that is expertly prepared. Restaurants are where we can enjoy an outing with friends and family, conduct business in a less-stuffy environment than a drab conference room, or have an intimate moment with someone we care deeply about.

Small local independent restaurants offer us an opportunity to sample the flavors of distant lands without having to travel to another country. They are a window into the soul of another culture and a way for all of us to find some semblance of unity in a bitterly divided world.

As a society, we need restaurants not just to survive – but to thrive. In fact, we need restaurants now more than ever before. Notwithstanding the economic benefits they provide our local communities, the sobering truth is that nowadays, a large segment of the population simply cannot cook. Even worse, they lack the skills to properly shop for wholesome ingredients to make nutritious meals at home.

It seems that over the past five decades or so, we have lost our way as a society. We have gradually prioritized the pursuit of fun and entertainment – over necessary life skills such as learning to cook, clean, or change a flat tire. Since the late 1970's, dual-income families have become the norm, frequently leaving practical skills such as cooking in the shadows.

Now, I won't get into a personal diatribe here, but suffice it to say that you have something truly special if you are a small restaurant owner. Something worth saving. Something worth sharing. Something worth preserving.

This, my friend, is why I do what I do.

Okay, moving on.

Table Turnover in a Post-Pandemic World

As I sit down to write this book in late 2023, I am reminded that while consumer preferences and attitudes have been gradually shifting for decades, the COVID-19 pandemic upended all of our lives in just a few short months. In fact, the entire restaurant industry has faced unprecedented challenges over a very short amount of time.

In the wake of the pandemic, small restaurants, in particular, have had to adapt – rethinking business models, sanitation practices, and customer engagement strategies. While delicious food remains at the heart of your establishment, it's time to also shift your focus beyond the food and pay close attention to the operational aspects of your restaurant. Ignoring this critical facet can be a costly mistake.

In today's competitive environment, surviving and thriving requires a holistic approach. Exceptional meals are just one part of the equation. You must also master the art of efficient restaurant operations, including the art of table turnover.

Table turnover is the rate at which tables in your restaurant become available for new guests. Think of it as the heartbeat or pulse of your establishment. It is a measure of your restaurant's efficiency in serving customers and directly impacts your profitability. The more efficiently you can turn tables without compromising the dining experience, the more revenue your restaurant can generate.

You may wonder why this matters so much. The answer lies in the numbers: industry research shows that increasing your table turnover rate by just a few percentage points can significantly boost your bottom line. But this isn't just about making more money in the short term; it's about ensuring your restaurant's long-term success and sustainability.

By the end of this book, you'll be armed with the knowledge and strategies needed to avoid the five most critical table turnover mistakes that many restaurant owners make. If left unaddressed, these mistakes will hinder your restaurant's growth, profitability, and customer satisfaction.

An Overview of What's In the Book

The goal of this book is to help you lay the foundation for long-term success in the fiercely competitive restaurant space. In the following chapters, we will meticulously dissect each of the five critical table turnover mistakes that can threaten your restaurant's growth and profitability.

In Chapters 2 and 3, we'll lay the foundation for why the majority of small restaurant owners don't take the time to look closely at their operations. We'll take a deep dive into the psychology behind this by discussing latent vs. patent mistakes and situational blindness.

In Chapters 4 through 8, we'll discuss the following 5 table turnover mistakes:

1. Poor Reservation Management. When handled incorrectly, this can lead to disorganized seating, customer dissatisfaction, and lost revenue. Ineffective reservation systems may result in overbookings or underbookings, disrupting your restaurant's flow and profitability.

2. Slow Service and Kitchen Delays. The second pitfall is slow service and kitchen delays. Lengthy wait times irritate diners, often prompting them to leave before finishing their meals. This can tarnish your restaurant's reputation and erode customer loyalty.

3. Poor Seating Optimization. Incorrect table arrangements, oversized tables, or suboptimal layouts can lead to inefficient use of space, hindering your ability to accommodate more guests. Addressing these inefficiencies is crucial for improving your restaurant's bottom line.

4. Poor Waitlist Management. Mishandling guests waiting for a table can result in frustration, negative online reviews, and potential customer loss. Effective waitlist management is one key to preserving your restaurant's positive reputation.

5. Poor Menu Presentation. Lastly, cluttered, confusing menus can lead to indecision and longer ordering times. Your menu should entice, inform, and streamline the ordering process.

In Chapter 9, we discuss staff training, customer service, and the impact that your staff has not only on your table turnover rate but also on forming memorable impressions of your restaurant in the minds of your diners.

In Chapters 10 and 11, we discuss the role of technology as the binding agent in helping to ensure smooth operations. Today's restaurant management systems are more than credit-card machines – they can help support a robust and efficient table turnover rate.

In Chapter 12, we'll cover some miscellaneous topics, including Social Media, Reputation Management, and Data Privacy.

Armed with knowledge, strategies, and practical insights, you will be well-equipped to transform your restaurant into a well-coordinated entity that excels both in the kitchen and in guest service. Are you prepared to embark on this journey toward operational excellence and increased profitability?

Great.

Let's go.

Chapter 2
Patent vs. Latent Mistakes: Unmasking the Unseen

"There are things known and there are things unknown, and in between are the doors of perception."

Aldous Huxley

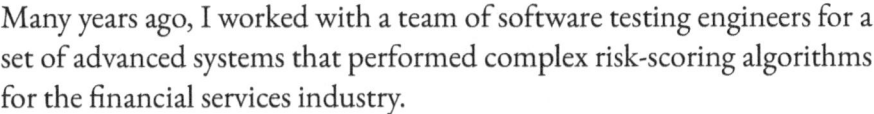

Many years ago, I worked with a team of software testing engineers for a set of advanced systems that performed complex risk-scoring algorithms for the financial services industry.

The software took hundreds of pieces of information about a person, combined it with information from other sources, and generated a score based on the risk that person posed to the company. There were hundreds of billions of possible combinations.

What's the point?

Well, in troubleshooting the output of a system like this, you'll see two types of errors. The first type of error is a system-generated error. Something obviously didn't go right. Either an invalid combination was generated, a piece of information wasn't entered, or something else went wrong.

The second type of error was much more insidious and complex. It was the case where a score was generated without error, but it was incorrect.

So, how do you test a system with billions of possible combinations?

How do you know which result is correct?

Without going into all of the geeky, gory details of how we went about solving this problem, the point here is that there were only two types of errors. The first was a "patent" error – or one fairly obvious to identify. The second one is a "latent" error – one that can lie dormant, unrecognized – and is much more difficult to spot.

Remember, the true nature of all business is problem-solving, whether you're an investment banker on Wall Street, a software engineer, or running a restaurant. Your objective is to solve problems for both your customers and your company. However, before you can solve a problem, you must first recognize it – and to do that, you need to acknowledge that what you're seeing is actually a problem.

As we prepare to dive into the specifics of the five critical table turnover mistakes, it's important to understand what sets subtle errors apart from the more obvious, or "patent," mistakes. We refer to these as "latent" mistakes—often concealed beneath the surface, lurking in the shadows, and quietly eroding your restaurant's success.

Let's start with the patent mistakes.

Patent Mistakes: The Obvious Blunders

Patent mistakes are the errors in a restaurant that are impossible to ignore, stand out like a sore thumb, and demand immediate action. These obvious blunders starkly contrast the subtlety of latent mistakes.

Here are some defining characteristics:

- **Immediate Visibility:** Patent mistakes are immediately visible to both restaurant staff and customers. For example, if a server spills a drink on a guest's lap, it's a glaring mishap that demands immediate attention. Customers and staff are acutely aware of what went wrong.

- **Prompt Response:** The very nature of patent mistakes necessitates swift responses. When a patent mistake occurs, it's typically addressed right away.

- **Tangible Consequences:** The consequences of patent mistakes are often tangible and easily quantifiable. A customer's dissatisfaction may result in a comped meal or a discounted bill. Staff may receive immediate constructive feedback or even disciplinary action.

- **Direct Customer Impact:** Patent mistakes can directly and immediately impact the customer's experience. A poorly prepared dish, an incorrect order, or a rude server can leave a lasting negative impression and lead to lost business.

- **Immediate Opportunities for Improvement:** While patent mistakes can be embarrassing, they also offer immediate opportunities for improvement. They serve as clear indicators of what went wrong and can lead to process improvements, additional training, or changes in procedures.

- **Reputation Management:** Managing patent mistakes effectively is crucial for maintaining a restaurant's reputation. A swift and sincere response to such errors can often turn a negative experience into a positive one, demonstrating the restaurant's commitment to customer satisfaction.

In sum, patent mistakes in a restaurant are the overt, unmistakable blunders that demand immediate attention. While they can be disruptive to the customer experience, they also offer clear opportunities for improvement. Correcting patent mistakes quickly provides a clear roadmap to easy wins.

Okay, let's move on to latent mistakes.

Latent Mistakes: The Silent Success Killers

Now, let's shift our focus to latent mistakes. These are the hidden, less obvious errors that evade immediate detection. Latent mistakes can quietly compromise your restaurant's efficiency, profitability, and reputation over time.

The five critical table turnover mistakes fall into the category of latent mistakes because they are not immediately apparent.

Here's why latent mistakes silently erode success:

Gradual Accumulation

Gradual accumulation is a defining characteristic of latent mistakes. Understanding how these mistakes develop is essential for recognizing their long-term impact on your restaurant's internal operations.

Here's a closer look at this phenomenon:

- **Incremental Shifts:** Latent mistakes often emerge through incremental shifts in operations or practices. These shifts may be so subtle that they go unnoticed for a while. For example, slight changes in kitchen workflow, guest seating protocols, or reservation management may not immediately register as problematic.

- **Unseen Consequences:** As these incremental shifts occur, they often come with unintended consequences that remain hidden. For instance, a minor change in kitchen processes might initially seem like an efficiency improvement. Still, over time, it could lead to increased kitchen delays, affecting the overall dining experience.

- **Delayed Impact:** The effects of gradual accumulation may take weeks, months, or even years. This delay in impact can make these mistakes challenging to identify since the cause-and-effect relationship is not readily apparent.

- **Creeping Inefficiency:** Latent mistakes are akin to a creeping inefficiency that quietly infiltrates a restaurant's operations. It's like a slow leak that, over time, can cause significant damage if left unaddressed.

- **Multiple Factors:** Latent mistakes often result from the interplay of multiple factors. They are not singular, isolated errors but the culmination of various elements converging in a way that disrupts the restaurant's harmony. Identifying and addressing each contributing factor can be complex and time-consuming.

- **Operational Blind Spots:** Because these mistakes develop so gradually and involve complex interactions, they can create operational blind spots. Restaurant owners may not recognize them until their collective impact becomes unmistakable.

- **Proactive Vigilance:** Mitigating the impact of gradual accumulation requires proactive vigilance. It involves regularly assessing and analyzing various operational aspects, even when they appear to be functioning adequately.

In essence, gradual accumulation is how latent mistakes silently take root and grow within a restaurant's operations. Recognizing this process is the first step in addressing these latent mistakes effectively.

Closely linked with gradual accumulation are complex interactions. Let's see how this plays into latent mistakes.

Complex Interactions

As you're well aware, a restaurant is a fast-paced operation with many moving parts. Interactions within a restaurant can converge in unexpected ways, leading to operational inefficiencies and challenges. Understanding complex interactions is crucial to spotting latent mistakes.

Here are some additional aspects:

- **Interconnected Elements:** Your restaurant is a dynamic ecosystem with interconnected elements, from kitchen operations to reservation management to waitstaff procedures. Each element can affect and be affected by others, creating a delicate balance.

- **Cause-and-effect Relationships:** Complex interactions often involve intricate cause-and-effect relationships. A seemingly minor change in one aspect of restaurant operations can trigger a cascade of effects throughout the entire process. For instance, modifying seating arrangements can impact kitchen workflow and service efficiency.

- **Chain Reactions:** One action can set off a chain reaction of events. This can lead to unforeseen consequences that, over time, contribute to latent mistakes. For example, a delay in service may result in rushed kitchen preparations, which, in turn, affect food quality.

- **Feedback Loops:** Complex interactions can create feedback loops, where an effect becomes a cause that further amplifies the initial problem. In the context of table turnover, a backlog of reservations can lead to service delays, resulting in frustrated guests and negative online reviews, perpetuating the issue.

- **Multifaceted Challenges:** Latent mistakes often arise from multifaceted challenges that defy simple solutions. They require a nuanced understanding of how various elements interact to create the problem. Addressing these challenges often demands a comprehensive approach – in some cases, a 3rd party trained in operational efficiency.

- **Operational Crossroads:** At the intersection of these complex interactions lies a potential operational crossroads. This is where the fate of a restaurant's success is decided, as the convergence of factors either enhances operational efficiency or hinders it.

- **Diagnostic Complexity:** Identifying latent mistakes rooted in complex interactions can be challenging. It often necessitates in-depth analysis, data collection, and a deep understanding of how different aspects of the restaurant interplay.

In essence, complex interactions underscore why latent mistakes are often elusive. They highlight the need for a holistic approach to problem-solving and an awareness of how even seemingly minor adjustments can trigger unforeseen consequences.

As we continue throughout the book, keep in mind that understanding these complex interactions is key to finding effective solutions and optimizing your restaurant's performance.

Lack of Immediate Feedback

Another distinguishing characteristic of latent mistakes is the lack of immediate feedback. In contrast to patent mistakes, where the consequences are readily apparent and often lead to immediate corrective action, latent mistakes often develop in a more subtle manner, without clear and immediate indicators. Understanding the implications of this is vital in comprehending why latent mistakes persist.

Here's a closer examination:

- **Invisible Consequences:** Latent mistakes often originate from actions or conditions that do not have immediately visible consequences. This makes it challenging for restaurant staff to recognize them in real-time. For instance, over time, poor reservation management may lead to missed revenue opportunities, but knowing how much money you're ***not*** making is difficult.

- **Unseen Guest Reactions:** Since latent mistakes do not trigger immediate guest complaints or reactions, they can easily fly under the radar. Guests may not vocalize their dissatisfaction at the moment, making it difficult for restaurant management to gauge the severity of the issue.

- **Operational Blind Spots:** The lack of immediate feedback can create operational blind spots. Restaurant owners often believe everything is running smoothly because they do not receive complaints or negative feedback from guests, even though latent mistakes are silently eroding profitability and guest satisfaction.

- **Cumulative Impact:** Latent mistakes, over time, can accumulate into significant problems. The gradual nature of these mistakes makes it challenging to pinpoint the exact moment when they began and when their impact became substantial.

- **Proactive Vigilance:** Recognizing latent mistakes requires proactive vigilance. It entails regularly assessing various operational aspects, even when there are no overt signs of trouble. Many small restaurant owners simply don't invest the time for this – they're off to the next emergency.

The lack of immediate feedback contributes to the persistence and subtlety of latent mistakes. It underscores the importance of proactive monitoring, analysis, and a holistic approach to restaurant management.

Let's move on to the most beguiling aspect of latent mistakes . . . apparent success.

The "Golden Blindfold": When Apparent Success Masks Critical Mistakes

Now that we've defined latent mistakes and outlined some of the core components, let's examine a big reason why some latent mistakes never get identified and remedied. Quite frequently, when a restaurant achieves some measure of success, a phenomenon that I like to refer to as the *"Golden Blindfold"* sets in.

What do I mean?

Well, success for many small restaurant owners becomes a blind spot — which is why they never grow and scale. They often reason, "*Well, we must be doing **something** right!*" So, they keep right down the same path day after day, year after year – staying the same, or, even worse, watching profits slowly erode without taking the time to discover why.

The real danger in this thinking lies in the fact that while they're focused on day-to-day operations, they fail to take note of the world changing around them. They exist only in the "bubble" they've created for themselves.

Let's examine this in a bit more detail.

Masked by Success

The fact that latent mistakes are often masked by success highlights a paradoxical aspect of the restaurant industry. Despite operational inefficiencies or critical mistakes, a restaurant may still appear to thrive on the surface due to other positive results.

Here are some examples:

- **Culinary Distraction:** Restaurants known for exceptional cuisine may inadvertently divert attention away from operational shortcomings. For a time, customers may focus primarily on the food, overlooking issues in service or other areas. These are often referred to as "*dives*" or "*hidden gems*" in a neighborhood.

- **Positive Word-of-mouth:** Successful restaurants often enjoy positive word-of-mouth recommendations based on their food. This positive buzz can overshadow underlying operational challenges despite attracting some new customers.

- **Customer Loyalty:** Even in the presence of latent mistakes, loyal customers who have experienced exceptional meals may continue to patronize the restaurant. Their loyalty can create the illusion of overall success.

- **Revenue Flow:** High demand for a restaurant's cuisine can mask revenue loss due to operational inefficiencies. The steady flow of customers may give the impression of prosperity even when profits are not maximized.

- **Online Reputation:** Restaurants with a strong culinary reputation may have positive online reviews that emphasize food quality while downplaying other aspects. This can often mislead potential customers about the overall dining experience.

- **Long-Term Sustainability:** Success in the short-term can obscure long-term sustainability. Operational mistakes may not immediately impact profitability but erode profitability over time as market conditions change.

- **Operational Blindness:** When success overshadows latent mistakes, restaurant management may become complacent and fail to address underlying issues. They may not even recognize the need for operational improvements until it's too late.

- **Quality vs. Consistency:** A successful restaurant may excel in delivering high-quality dishes but struggle with consistency. Latent mistakes can lead to variations in service quality, which may go unnoticed among customers who don't visit regularly.

Latent mistakes can thrive in an environment where positive attributes overshadow operational inefficiencies. As we continue into each of the five critical table turnover mistakes, keep in mind that the possibility of apparent success masking underlying issues is a reality.

Now, let's dive into a few of these aspects in more detail.

Overemphasis on Culinary Perfection

To be sure, culinary excellence is a coveted hallmark of restaurant success. While a commitment to culinary perfection is commendable, it can, at times, lead to inadvertently missing other crucial operational aspects.

Here's a deeper look:

- Obsession with the Plate: Restaurant owners and chefs passionate about their cuisine may fixate on perfecting each dish. This dedication can drive culinary innovation, but it can also create tunnel vision, where the plate takes center stage, and other elements are overshadowed or ignored.

- **Guest Expectations:** When a restaurant earns a reputation for culinary excellence, customers naturally have high expectations. Therefore, exceeding these expectations becomes paramount. This intense focus on satisfying the diner's palate can lead to neglect in other areas, such as service efficiency or reservation management.

- **Positive Reinforcement:** Success in the culinary realm is often met with immediate and tangible positive reinforcement. Customer compliments, glowing reviews, and repeat business all highlight and validate the restaurant's culinary prowess. This positive feedback loop can reinforce the false belief that culinary excellence alone is sufficient for long-term success.

- **Culinary Creativity vs. Operational Oversight:** The creative process of developing new dishes and refining existing ones can consume significant time and energy. This may inadvertently divert attention and valuable resources away from operational oversight and improvement. The operational side of the business becomes a blind spot.

- **Singular Definition of Success:** In some cases, culinary excellence is perceived as the sole indicator of a restaurant's success. If the food consistently delights diners, other operational challenges may be downplayed or overlooked because they do not align with this singular definition.

- **Risk of Complacency:** A successful culinary track record can lead to a sense of complacency. If the restaurant is thriving due to culinary excellence, there may be a reluctance to make changes or investments in other areas. Situational blindness often sets in as the focus remains on what has worked in the past.

- **Operational Neglect:** As restaurant leadership becomes consumed with culinary perfection, operational challenges, such as slow service or poor reservation management, may persist unnoticed. These issues can hinder overall guest satisfaction, even if the food continues to shine.

The overemphasis on culinary excellence can be a double-edged sword. While it drives innovation, customer loyalty, and praise, it can also lead to situational blindness regarding the operational aspects of the restaurant.

Recognizing the need for a balanced approach—one that values both culinary and operational excellence—is essential to ensure your restaurant's ability to effectively address latent mistakes.

Customer Satisfaction and Positive Reviews

Conventional wisdom tells small business owners that *"The customer is always right."*

So, in their pursuit of excellence, restaurant owners and managers often view customer satisfaction as the ultimate priority. While ensuring diners leave happy and content is undeniably important, an exclusive focus on this aspect can inadvertently become a distraction in itself, leading to situational blindness when it comes to other operational considerations.

Here's a deeper exploration of how customer satisfaction can divert attention from other crucial areas:

- **Pursuit of Positive Reviews:** Positive customer reviews, both online and through word-of-mouth, are powerful tools for attracting new business. Consequently, many restaurants place great emphasis on maintaining high ratings. This emphasis can inadvertently create a narrow focus on ensuring customer satisfaction in the short term, possibly at the expense of long-term operational efficiency.

- **Immediate Feedback as the Measure of Success:** Immediate customer feedback provides instant gratification and positive reinforcement. It can lead to the belief that as long as customers are happy at the moment, the restaurant is thriving. This myopic focus on immediate reactions can obscure latent operational challenges.

- **Operational Challenges as Secondary:** When a restaurant is consistently praised for customer satisfaction, operational challenges may be perceived as secondary concerns. Managers and staff may be less inclined to address issues such as service speed, reservation management, or table turnover optimization because the immediate customer experience appears to be satisfactory.

- **Customer-Centric Decision-Making:** A customer-centric approach to decision-making can sometimes lead to decisions that prioritize individual guest preferences over overall operational efficiency. For example, accommodating last-minute reservation requests to satisfy a single guest may disrupt the restaurant's seating plan and service flow.

- **Maintenance vs. Innovation:** Focusing on maintaining high levels of customer satisfaction can divert resources away from innovation and operational improvements. Restaurant owners may be more inclined to maintain the status quo rather than invest in changes that might enhance long-term efficiency.

- **The Perceived Success Trap:** Continuous positive feedback and a loyal customer base can create the illusion of success. This perception can lead to complacency regarding latent operational mistakes. If everything seems to be going well in the eyes of customers, it may be assumed that there's no need for change.

While customer satisfaction is a cornerstone of restaurant success, it can distract from other critical operational considerations when focused on exclusively. Recognizing the balance between satisfying immediate customer needs and addressing long-term operational efficiency is essential for proactively addressing latent mistakes in restaurant management.

Complacency with Limited Success

Success can be both a blessing and a curse for restaurants. When a restaurant is thriving and receiving praise for its food, there is a temptation to become complacent, assuming that what has worked so far will continue to do so – even when the market or customer preferences change. Complacency can easily cause operational challenges and latent mistakes to be overlooked or grossly underestimated.

Here's a closer look at how complacency can develop and its implications:

- **Assumption of a Winning Formula:** When a restaurant experiences prolonged success, there's a natural inclination to attribute that success to a particular formula. This formula might involve a signature dish, a specific ambiance, or a particular style of service. The assumption that this formula is infallible can lead to complacency.

- **Resistance to Change:** Complacency often manifests itself as resistance to change. Since the current approach has yielded success, there is often a reluctance to make adjustments or improvements. This can extend to operational aspects of the restaurant, such as table turnover, reservation management, or waitlist optimization.

- **Focus on Preservation, Not Enhancement:** Complacency tends to prioritize preservation over enhancement. Rather than actively seeking ways to improve the restaurant's operations, management may be content with maintaining the status quo. This focus on preservation can inadvertently blind decision-makers to latent mistakes.

- **Failure to Innovate:** A successful restaurant may see innovation as unnecessary. If things are going relatively well, there may be little incentive to innovate or introduce new practices. This stagnation can lead to the perpetuation of latent mistakes that might have otherwise been addressed.

- **Loss of Competitive Edge:** Complacency can result in a loss of the competitive edge that initially drove the restaurant's success. Rival establishments may be more agile in adapting to changing customer preferences or addressing operational challenges, gradually eroding the restaurant's market share.

- **Operational Challenges Unaddressed:** Operational challenges, including those related to table turnover, seating optimization, or reservation management, may persist due to complacency. The restaurant's leadership may underestimate the significance of these issues, believing that they are inconsequential when compared to culinary excellence.

- **Customer Perception:** While customers may continue to patronize a restaurant due to its culinary reputation, they may gradually notice operational inefficiencies. Over time, this can impact their overall perception of the dining experience and gradually lead to attrition.

- **Risk Aversion:** The fear of disrupting a winning formula or taking risks can lead to the inhibition of change. Managers and owners may worry that introducing new practices or making operational adjustments could jeopardize the restaurant's reputation or customer loyalty.

- **Change in Customer Expectations:** Customer preferences and expectations can evolve over time. Complacency may cause a restaurant to fall out of sync with these evolving expectations, leading to a disconnect between what the restaurant offers and what customers desire.

Complacency is a common pitfall for restaurants that have achieved acclaim, leading to a reluctance to address operational challenges and latent mistakes. Recognizing the importance of continual improvement and the dynamic nature of the industry is crucial for avoiding complacency and sustaining long-term success beyond the initial formula.

In the next chapter, we'll define and take a closer look at situational blindness — another reason why latent mistakes often thrive.

Chapter 3
Seeing the Bigger Picture: From Situational Blindness to Operational Clarity

> *"You will always define events in a manner which will validate your agreement with reality."*
>
> Steve Maraboli

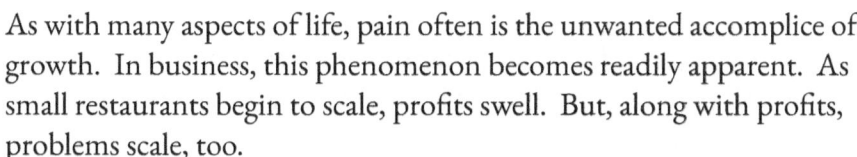

As with many aspects of life, pain often is the unwanted accomplice of growth. In business, this phenomenon becomes readily apparent. As small restaurants begin to scale, profits swell. But, along with profits, problems scale, too.

In the last chapter, we alluded to situational blindness quite a bit, so in this chapter, we'll define what it is, how it can obscure latent problems, and how those problems become more evident as you grow.

First, let's take a moment to define situational blindness.

Situational blindness is a cognitive phenomenon where individuals fail to perceive or fully comprehend critical information in a particular situation, even though that information is clearly available.

It can lead to decision-making errors, missed opportunities, and the inability to recognize important cues. In essence, situational blindness occurs when individuals are so focused on one problem (or, certain aspects of a problem) that they overlook or neglect other crucial problems.

While situational blindness can exist in restaurants of any size, it is found more frequently in smaller restaurants. Let's explore the phenomenon of situational blindness while also taking a look at some of the scaling challenges that often force small restaurant owners to address situational blindness as latent problems begin to come into full view.

Situational Blindness in Small Restaurants

In smaller restaurant operations, situational blindness is common; concealing latent mistakes and operational inefficiencies. Quite often, this phenomenon exists under the guise of manageable operations and limited customer volume.

However, as a restaurant gains more customers or attempts to scale up its operations, the flaws that were once hidden beneath the surface can suddenly become glaringly apparent.

While growth brings obvious financial rewards, transitioning from a small-scale to a larger-scale operation can also serve as a magnifying glass, revealing the consequences of previously overlooked mistakes.

Most notably, small restaurants' limited customer volume, personalized service, and flexible operations are common characteristics that often limit situational awareness.

Let's examine each of these aspects in turn.

Limited Customer Volume

Limited customer volume is a factor that can contribute to situational blindness. While this may seem inconsequential, it plays a pivotal role in concealing latent mistakes and operational inefficiencies.

Here's how:

Cozy Atmosphere

Small restaurants often boast an intimate and cozy atmosphere. This setting creates an illusion of exclusivity and charm, which can positively influence the perception of the dining experience. Customers may associate limited seats with an intimate ambiance and personalized service.

A cozy ambiance and personalized service generally invoke feelings of being part of an exclusive group. Not surprisingly, customers dining in small restaurants generally perceive the dining experience positively. As a result, they may overlook minor operational hiccups or inefficiencies.

> Additionally, this can lead to what I like to refer to as the "*our special place*" syndrome – where customers who enjoy the cozy atmosphere and unique ambiance don't tell others because they want to keep it cozy (and scarce).
>
> They fear that as word spreads and crowds form, there will be a longer wait, and the quality of the food may even suffer. Thus, their cozy little-known hideaway will disappear. So, they purposely don't share their experience with others, which hurts the restaurant's bottom line (especially if it exclusively relies on word-of-mouth promotion).

Perceived Manageability

The restaurant's management and staff may perceive operations as manageable with a smaller customer base. They might erroneously believe they can easily handle reservations, seating arrangements, and service without needing advanced systems or strategies.

This perception of manageability can easily lead to complacency. In small restaurants, many operational processes are often managed manually. Reservations may be recorded in a notebook or, worse yet, post-it notes, and seating arrangements may be handled informally. At first glance, these manual methods can appear sufficient, masking the need for more sophisticated systems.

High Staff-to-Customer Ratio

Small restaurants may have a relatively high staff-to-customer ratio, allowing for more attentive and personalized service. Waitstaff can afford to "invest" time chatting with and building relationships with regulars – anticipating their preferences and providing a level of attention that larger establishments may not be able to match.

In turn, regulars appreciate the personalized service and, over time, build a sense of loyalty to the restaurant. However, this can lead to a restaurant's bottom line being almost entirely supported by a few regular customers. Even worse, if a management change occurs or a popular staff member quits, then customer loyalty can quickly evaporate, leading to devastating financial consequences.

It's important to remember that situational blindness caused by the apparent benefits of limited customer volume begins to fade quickly as a restaurant grows or attempts to scale its operations. What once seemed manageable can quickly become a challenge, and the latent mistakes that were concealed by this limited volume quickly begin to surface.

Let's move on to personalized service.

Personalized Service

One of the distinguishing features of small restaurants is the ability to provide genuine, personalized service to each guest. While this level of attention enhances the dining experience, it also contributes to situational blindness.

Here's a more detailed exploration of how this plays out:

- **High Staff-to-Customer Ratio:** Small restaurants often maintain a high staff-to-customer ratio, which allows waitstaff to focus on individual guests. This personalized approach enables staff to build relationships, remember guest preferences, and anticipate their needs.

- **Individualized Attention:** Waitstaff can provide more individualized attention to each table in small restaurants. This may involve conversing with diners, offering recommendations, and accommodating special requests. Guests often appreciate this level of engagement, which can overshadow minor operational delays.

- **Guest Recognition:** Staff often recognize and remember frequent diners in small restaurants. This recognition fosters a sense of familiarity and a welcoming atmosphere. Guests feel valued when they are acknowledged and remembered from previous visits.

- **Expedited Problem Resolution:** When issues or complaints arise, personalized service allows staff to address them promptly. Staff members are empowered to resolve problems on the spot, mitigating the impact of any operational issues.

- **Positive Guest Perceptions:** Guests in small restaurants tend to have positive perceptions of the dining experience due to the attentive service and personal touch. They may be more forgiving of minor operational hiccups because they prioritize the overall atmosphere and the feeling of being well-cared for on a consistent basis.

- **Enhanced Dining Experience:** The individualized attention and personalized service contribute to an enhanced dining experience. This can lead customers to focus on the quality of the food and the friendly service while potentially overlooking operational hiccups.

While personalized service generally enhances the dining experience in small restaurants, it can also allow situational blindness to set in, further contributing to the low visibility of latent operational mistakes. As a restaurant grows or expands, finding the right balance between personalized service and operational efficiency becomes essential to maintaining the high standards that guests expect while addressing hidden challenges.

Operational Flexibility

Operational flexibility refers to a restaurant's ability to adapt and respond to changing circumstances, customer demands, and unforeseen challenges. While flexibility is often seen as a strength, it can also serve as a double-edged sword, particularly when it comes to allowing situational blindness to set in.

Here's how flexible operations impact small restaurants:

- **Adaptability to Customer Preferences:** Small restaurants generally have the advantage of swiftly adapting to customer preferences. If a particular dish gains popularity or if dietary trends change, menus can quickly adjust to evolving tastes. However, this flexibility can sometimes mask latent menu planning and cost management mistakes. Restaurant owners may fail to recognize that frequent menu changes can impact kitchen efficiency, inventory management, and staff training.

- **Informal Operational Processes:** Flexibility also leads to informal operational processes. Staff members may rely on their experience and intuition rather than following established guidelines and protocols. While this informality can contribute to a warm and personalized guest experience, it can also contribute to situational blindness related to consistency, training, and communication. Over time, inconsistencies manifest themselves when multiple staff members handle the same task differently.

- **Handling Rush Hours:** Flexible operations enable small restaurants to handle fluctuations in customer traffic, especially during peak hours. Staff members may multitask and adapt to the ebb and flow of guests. However, this adaptability can obscure latent mistakes related to staffing levels, resource allocation, and service speed. During busy periods, the restaurant may inadvertently compromise on guest satisfaction, leading to long wait times and service mistakes.

- **Dealing with Special Requests:** Small restaurants often go to great lengths to accommodate special requests from guests, such as dietary restrictions or customizing menu items. While this personalized service can create a positive impression, it can also result in operational mistakes. Servers may fail to communicate special requests accurately with the kitchen, leading to errors in food preparation. Additionally, an overemphasis on customization can strain kitchen resources and cause delays.

- **Ad-Hoc Decision-Making:** Small restaurant owners and staff are often known for their ability to make quick decisions. This agility allows them to address issues promptly and satisfy guest needs on the spot. However, an overreliance on quick decision-making can mask mistakes in process optimization. The restaurant may not recognize that certain operational processes could be streamlined to improve efficiency and guest satisfaction.

While flexible operations are a hallmark of small restaurants, they can lead to situational blindness – inadvertently hiding latent mistakes and operational inefficiencies. Recognizing the fine line between adaptability and potential pitfalls is crucial. By striking a balance between flexibility and the need for structured operational processes, your restaurant can ensure consistent service quality, enhance guest satisfaction, and address hidden mistakes as they continue to grow.

Growth Pains & Scaling Challenges

Let's start with a not-so-obvious distinction between growth and scaling. Growth can be either intentional or non-intentional. However, scaling is always intentional. It is important to realize that latent problems that are ignored due to situational blindness can begin to manifest themselves during either process or both.

When a small restaurant begins to grow in popularity, it is undoubtedly a happy time. More money means more opportunities to buy in bulk, invest in better equipment, and develop and train your staff. However, it also brings several challenges. In this section, we'll dive into some of those operational challenges that begin to surface.

Higher Customer Volume

Small restaurants are generally characterized by limited seating capacity and, consequently, a manageable flow of customers. However, when they experience an increase in customer volume due to popularity or expansion, it can significantly impact operations and reveal latent mistakes that were previously concealed.

Here's a more detailed look at this phenomenon.

- **Logistical Challenges:** As customer volume grows, the logistical challenges associated with seating, service, and kitchen operations become more pronounced. The once-manageable flow of patrons can become a complex puzzle requiring efficient solutions.

- **Table Turnover:** Small restaurants may not emphasize table turnover when customer volume is low. With higher volume, the need for quicker table turnover becomes evident to accommodate waiting guests. Latent mistakes related to table turnover efficiency become more apparent.

- **Reservation Management:** When small restaurants gain popularity, the demand for reservations naturally increases. Mistakes in reservation management, such as overbooking or inadequate allocation of tables, can lead to longer wait times and dissatisfied guests.

- **Lack of personalization:** Providing the same level of personalized service becomes increasingly challenging as more customers (with varying personalities and expectations) appear. Generally speaking, staff levels cannot always scale proportionately to growth because other operational costs begin to set in. Waitstaff may struggle to keep up with individual needs and preferences, leading to the risk of poor service.

- **Waitlist Optimization:** Having a waitlist during peak hours is a common consequence of increased customer volume. Mistakes in waitlist management, such as inaccurate wait time estimates or insufficient communication, can negatively impact the guest experience.

- **Staff Overwhelm:** The surge in customer volume can overwhelm staff, leading to service delays and reduced attentiveness. Operational mistakes may include inadequate staffing levels, insufficient training, or the absence of clear workflows to handle increased demand.

- **Quality Control:** A restaurant's ability to maintain the quality of food and service can be challenged when faced with a sudden influx of guests. Operational mistakes that were previously manageable can then result in poor quality and guest dissatisfaction.

- **Customer Expectations:** As your customer base expands, so do expectations. Guests may expect the same level of quality and service they received when the restaurant had fewer customers. Operational inefficiencies can lead to unmet expectations and negative reviews – thus creating a downward spiral of lower guest satisfaction leading to lower revenue, and vice versa.

- **Revenue Opportunities:** While increased customer volume means more revenue, operational mistakes can hinder a restaurant's ability to capitalize on them. Mistakes related to efficiency, service speed, and guest satisfaction may result in missed revenue potential.

- **Online Reputation:** Latent mistakes exposed by increased volume can lead to negative online reviews and social media feedback. The restaurant's online reputation may be affected, deterring potential guests.

Increased customer volume is a double-edged sword for small restaurants. The flow of more customers means additional revenue and increased popularity. However, it also brings operational challenges to the forefront. Lack of situational awareness related to table turnover, reservation management, waitlist optimization, and service efficiency makes these problems more apparent and impactful, underscoring the need for proactive assessment and improvements to ensure a seamless dining experience.

Now, let's take a look at things from an operational standpoint.

Operational Complexity

Operational complexity arises as another consequence of increased customer volume and the need to adapt to the demands of a growing restaurant. Initially characterized by simplicity and informality, small restaurants face operational challenges as they scale up.

Here's how operational complexity, masked by situational blindness, can reveal latent mistakes when growing or scaling:

- **Advanced Systems and Tools:** To handle a larger customer base efficiently, small restaurants frequently need to implement advanced reservation systems, seating optimization tools, and waitlist management software. These technological solutions can expose gaps in existing operational processes, highlighting latent mistakes in the management of these systems.

- **Structured Workflows:** As customer flow increases, having structured workflows becomes essential. The need for well-defined roles and responsibilities becomes apparent, and operational mistakes in the absence of clear workflows can lead to confusion, delays, and guest dissatisfaction.

- **Staff Training and Management:** Scaling up necessitates hiring and training staff members. Operational mistakes related to staff training, management, and supervision may become evident as a larger team requires more structured and efficient guidance from management.

- **Communication Challenges:** With increased operational complexity, effective communication becomes paramount. Mistakes in communication, whether between front-of-house and back-of-house staff or among team members, can result in mismanagement, service errors, and guest complaints.

- **Quality and Consistency:** Maintaining consistent quality in both food and service also becomes more challenging as complexity increases. Operational mistakes that were previously manageable can now lead to lapses in quality, impacting the restaurant's reputation and guest satisfaction.

- **Resource Allocation:** Proper allocation of resources, including staff, time, and kitchen capacity, becomes crucial when managing a larger volume of guests. Mistakes in resource allocation can lead to operational bottlenecks, extended wait times, and guest dissatisfaction.

- **Adaptation to Peak Times:** As a restaurant scales, it must adapt to handle peak dining times efficiently. Operational mistakes during these high-demand periods, such as insufficient kitchen capacity or understaffing during peak hours, can result in service delays and frustrated diners.

- **Guest Experience Consistency:** Consistency in the guest experience becomes a greater challenge with operational complexity. Mistakes in delivering a consistent experience across various shifts and days of the week can diminish customer loyalty.

- **Pressure for Innovation:** Navigating operational complexity creates pressure for innovation. Restaurants often must adopt modern practices and technologies to streamline operations. Mistakes made during this transition can disrupt the flow of service and affect guest perception.

- **Risk Mitigation:** Operational complexity heightens the risk of unforeseen challenges, such as equipment failures, staff shortages, or supply chain disruptions. Restaurants need effective contingency plans and risk management strategies to mitigate the impact of these issues.

Operational complexity is a natural consequence of growth and increased customer volume. While it can reveal latent mistakes and inefficiencies, it also presents an opportunity for small restaurants to improve and refine their operational processes, implement advanced systems, and enhance staff training to ensure a seamless and consistent dining experience for all guests, regardless of the scale of the operation.

Hidden Operational Bottlenecks

Operational bottlenecks are points in a restaurant's processes where the flow of operations slows down or becomes obstructed, leading to delays in service and reduced efficiency. These bottlenecks are often hidden when restaurants are small but become more pronounced and problematic as the establishment scales up or experiences increased customer volume.

Operational complexity and bottlenecks are closely linked. When a restaurant's operational complexity increases, this frequently leads to bottlenecks if the underlying issues are not addressed proactively. In cases where situational blindness sets in, so do bottlenecks.

Here are some common causes of operational bottlenecks and their effects:

- **Seating and Table Turnover:** In small restaurants, seating and table turnover management may be relatively informal, and staff can handle it manually. However, this process can become a significant problem as the customer volume increases. Inefficient seating arrangements, slow table turnover, or inadequate reservation management can result in longer wait times for guests and lower revenue potential.

- **Kitchen Efficiency:** The kitchen is a critical area prone to bottlenecks, especially during peak dining hours. In small restaurants, the kitchen staff may adapt to the manageable volume of orders. However, as the restaurant scales, the kitchen may struggle to keep up with increased demand. Delays in food preparation, cooking, or plating result in longer wait times for diners.

- **Waitlist Management:** When a small restaurant experiences growth, there is generally a waitlist to manage guest arrivals during busy periods. However, the efficiency of the waitlist management process can become a bottleneck. Mistakes in waitlist coordination, inaccurate wait time estimates, or inadequate communication with waiting guests can lead to dissatisfaction.

- **Staffing Levels:** Small restaurants may have a lean staff, and this model can work well when the customer volume is low. However, as the restaurant scales, staffing levels may not be properly adjusted to meet the increased demand. Insufficient staff leads to delays in service, slower table turnover, and operational bottlenecks.

- **Communication Breakdowns:** Effective and efficient communication is crucial for restaurant operations. Small restaurants may rely on informal communication methods, but these can break down when dealing with larger volumes of guests. Miscommunication between staff members or between front-of-house and back-of-house teams can result in errors and service delays.

- **Resource Allocation:** Efficient allocation of resources, such as staff, kitchen equipment, and inventory, is essential for smooth operations. Small restaurants may not face significant challenges in this regard, but as the customer volume increases, mistakes in resource allocation can create bottlenecks. For example, inadequate kitchen capacity can lead to slower food preparation.

- **Quality Control:** Ensuring consistent quality in both food and service becomes more challenging as the restaurant scales up. Operational bottlenecks can lead to lapses in quality, impacting the guest experience and potentially causing dissatisfaction among customers.

- **Extended Wait Times:** Operational bottlenecks result in longer guest wait times, frustrating them, especially during peak hours. Extended wait times can lead to guest dissatisfaction and may deter repeat business.

- **Tarnished Online Reputation:** Negative experiences resulting from operational bottlenecks can lead to unfavorable online reviews and social media feedback. These reviews can tarnish a restaurant's online reputation, affecting its ability to attract new customers.

- **Revenue Loss:** Operational bottlenecks can directly impact revenue potential. Longer wait times, slower table turnover, and delays in service can result in missed revenue opportunities, affecting financial performance.

Recognizing and addressing operational bottlenecks is crucial to maintaining a positive guest experience, maximizing revenue potential, and achieving long-term success. As small restaurants grow or experience increased customer volume, they must invest in optimizing their processes, implementing efficient systems, and adapting to increased demands to minimize bottlenecks and ensure smooth operations.

Why Growing & Scaling Can Feel Overwhelming

As restaurants grow and scale, owners are commonly overwhelmed. They feel that they are not only climbing an uphill battle, but the mountain itself seems to grow steeper. Some fall into a state of despair without fully understanding that their mindset needs to change as their business evolves. They fail to realize that the framework for how their business operates is now obsolete. They are not failures but simply on the precipice of greater success.

What often happens is the visibility of latent mistakes, often hidden in the operational processes of a smaller restaurant (due to situational blindness), becomes much more apparent as the restaurant scales up or experiences increased customer volume. While these mistakes might go unnoticed in a smaller setting, they can significantly impact the guest experience and operational efficiency when brought to light.

Here's why:

- **Amplified Impact:** With a larger customer volume, the impact of operational mistakes is amplified. What might have been a minor inconvenience in a small restaurant can become a substantial disruption when experienced by a greater number of guests. For example, a delay in table turnover affects more diners during peak hours.

- **Guest Feedback:** As customer volume grows, so does the amount of feedback and reviews received by the restaurant. Negative experiences resulting from operational mistakes are more likely to be voiced by a larger pool of guests, making these mistakes more internally and externally visible.

- **Increased Complexity:** Scaling up often involves implementing more complex operational systems and processes. Introducing reservation systems, waitlist management software, and advanced seating optimization tools can highlight errors and inefficiencies in managing these systems. Additionally, it takes time for both management and staff to learn and adjust to the new procedures.

- **Higher Guest Expectations:** As the restaurant expands, guest expectations tend to rise. Customers expect a consistent level of service and quality, which can magnify the impact of operational mistakes. Even minor errors can result in guest dissatisfaction and tarnish the restaurant's reputation. The customer experience is no longer benchmarked against other small restaurants but, rather, larger ones that may have more mature processes.

- **Service Consistency:** Maintaining consistent service quality across different shifts, days, and levels of customer volume commonly becomes a challenge as the restaurant grows. Latent training, supervision, and communication issues become more apparent when there is a lack of service consistency.

- **Guest Wait Times:** Operational hiccups related to wait times for seating or service also become more visible as the restaurant scales. Longer wait times can lead to guest frustration and may be exacerbated during peak dining hours.

The visibility of latent mistakes increases as small restaurants grow or experience greater customer volume. These mistakes, which were previously hidden, can impact guest satisfaction, online reputation, and overall operational efficiency. Recognizing and addressing these mistakes becomes essential for maintaining a positive guest experience and achieving long-term success.

In the next section, we'll start exploring the 5 table turnover mistakes in detail. For now, remember that complexities related to growth and situational blindness can be contributing factors to why many of these mistakes persist.

SECTION 2

The 5 Table Turnover Mistakes

In this section, we get to the heart of our discussion — the 5 Table Turnover Mistakes. We'll examine each one in turn and discuss each mistake's potential impact and consequences.

We'll also provide actionable tips, strategies, and solutions that you can use to identify each of these mistakes and prevent them from sabotaging your restaurant.

Ready?

Great. Let's get started.

CHAPTER 4
Mistake #1: Poor Reservation Management

"If you don't have time to do it right, when will you have time to do it over?"

John Wooden

Our journey into the 5 table turnover mistakes starts with one that occurs even before your customers arrive at your restaurant – poor reservation management. In this chapter, we'll shed light on why it's more than just a minor hiccup in your restaurant's operations.

But first, what exactly is Reservation Management?

It's more than just scribbling down names in a reservation book or adding time slots to your online booking system. It encompasses a strategic and systematic approach to handling reservations that ensures the smooth operation of your establishment.

Industry experts often emphasize that efficient reservation management is a fundamental aspect of running a successful restaurant. It involves everything from reservation policies to staff training, and it directly impacts your restaurant's reputation and bottom line.

Consequences of Poor Reservation Management

Imagine your restaurant on a busy Saturday night. The vibe is simply electric. Your restaurant is buzzing with excitement, but the atmosphere eventually turns chaotic.

The problem?

Your tables are overbooked.

As a result, guests are waiting far longer than they should, and frustration fills the air. Poor Reservation Management can be a silent saboteur, and one of its most visible consequences is overcrowding and frustrated diners.

The Problem of Overcrowding

Overcrowding leads to an uncomfortable dining atmosphere, where guests may feel cramped and overlooked. It can cause irritated patrons to leave negative reviews which discourage potential future customers from visiting. When reservations are mismanaged, the inevitable consequence is overcrowding.

Here's what often happens:

- **Overbooked Tables:** Poor Reservation Management can lead to overbooked tables, where more reservations are accepted than your restaurant's physical space can accommodate.

- **Long Wait Times:** Guests, expecting to be seated promptly, are instead met with long wait times, forcing them to stand in crowded lobbies or hover near the entrance.

- **Reduced Comfort:** Overcrowding often diminishes guest comfort. Tables are often squeezed too close together, leading to an uncomfortable dining environment.

- **Negative First Impressions:** Overcrowding creates negative first impressions. Guests might interpret the crowded setting as a sign of disorganization or a lack of attention to detail.

The Frustration of Diners

Alongside overcrowding comes the frustration of diners, which can quickly escalate if not managed properly:

- **Impatience:** Waiting for a table beyond the expected reservation time can test the patience of even the most understanding guests.

- **Disappointment:** Guests who had high expectations for their dining experience may be disappointed by the initial inconvenience, which can color their perception of the entire meal.

- **Lost Business:** In some cases, the frustration can be so profound that it leads to lost business as guests vow never to return.

The consequences of overcrowding and frustrated diners extend beyond the immediate dining experience. They can damage your restaurant's reputation and quickly erode customer loyalty.

Let me end this section with a quick story. In the late 1990s and early 2000s, it was common for friends and family to want to go to big chain restaurants like The Olive Garden®, Red Lobster®, and others on a Friday or Saturday evening. However, I refused to patronize these restaurants.

The problem?

It was not uncommon to wait over 2 hours to be seated (even with a reservation).

Even back then, I simply refused to do it. There were better options with faster seating times. In fact, I'd rather pay more money for a better dining experience, knowing that my time is respected, than sit in a cold lobby waiting for a table to eat mediocre food.

Today, those restaurants are hardly a vestige of what they were back then, and a 2-hour wait is simply unacceptable now. It is important to remember that people are much more impatient than they were, say, 5 or 10 years ago. Society moves fast – and so must your restaurant. People have options, including delivery, meal prep services, and your competitors.

Why Poor Reservation Management Can't Be Ignored

Ignoring the issue of Poor Reservation Management can be costly in more ways than one. When reservations are mishandled, you may face several financial consequences:

- **Lost Revenue:** Empty tables due to overbooking or no-shows result in lost revenue. Every empty seat represents missed opportunities to earn money.

- **Negative Reviews:** Unhappy customers who experience reservation mishaps are more likely to leave negative reviews online. These reviews can often deter potential customers from choosing your restaurant – without giving you the opportunity to explain the situation.

- **Damage to Reputation:** In the competitive landscape, word of mouth can make or break a restaurant. A tarnished reputation can take several months to recover from, leading to decreased customer loyalty and a decline in business.

- **Wasted Resources:** Overstaffing to accommodate reservations that don't show up can lead to increased labor costs. Conversely, understaffing can result in poor service and a negative dining experience.

Understanding the consequences of Poor Reservation Handling is the first step in avoiding this critical mistake. Now, let's move on to some actionable tips and best practices to help you manage reservations efficiently to prevent these detrimental outcomes.

> "... it is said that the most expensive part of doing business in a restaurant is having empty seats." – CBC[1]

Reservation Management Best Practices

Now, let's turn our attention to some powerful strategies to help you streamline your reservation process. Effective reservation management prevents chaos and frustration from mishandled reservations and paves the way for a thriving restaurant.

Implement a Reservation System

The obvious first step in effective Reservation Management is implementing a reservation system. A spiral notebook just won't cut it in today's tech-driven world. In fact, a reservation system can be your restaurant's best friend. It simplifies the booking process and provides valuable data insights that can shape your business strategy.

Here are some additional benefits.

- **Streamlined Booking Process:** Reservation software makes it

---

1. https://www.cbc.ca/news/canada/kitchener-waterloo/andrew-coppolino-reservations-restaurant-no-shows-cancel-1.6712967

easy for customers to reserve a table, whether they're using your website, a third-party platform, or calling in. It removes the hassles of manual booking and reduces the risk of errors.

- **Improved Guest Experience:** Guests appreciate the convenience of making reservations online. They feel more in control of their dining experience, which often leads to higher satisfaction.

- **Data Insights:** Modern reservation systems provide valuable data on reservation patterns, customer preferences, and peak dining times. This data can guide intelligent decisions on staffing, menu offerings, and marketing strategies.

- **Reduced No-Shows:** Many reservation systems offer automated confirmation, reminder emails, and text messages, reducing the likelihood of no-shows and last-minute cancellations.

- **Efficient Table Management:** With real-time updates on reservations, your host or hostess can manage seating more efficiently, reducing wait times and ensuring a smoother flow of service.

How to Choose the Right Reservation System

Choosing the right reservation system for your restaurant is crucial. All salespeople promise the world, but few want to back up those promises over the long term. So, the critical task of picking the right system based on your operation and infrastructure is up to you.

Here are some considerations to help you through the process:

Research and Compare: Start by researching different reservation systems. Look for user reviews and ratings to gauge their reliability and user-friendliness.

Consider Your Needs: Identify your specific needs and budget. Some systems are tailored for small restaurants, while others are designed for larger establishments. Determine what features are essential for your business.

PRO TIP: If your restaurant is growing, consider implementing a system for a larger operation. It is better to go with a system that will cover your needs for the next 3-5 years than to have to upgrade in a hurry because a system is either obsolete or inadequate for the size of your restaurant.

- **Demo and Trial:** Don't hesitate to request in-house demos or free trials. This hands-on experience will help you and your staff assess if the system aligns with your operational requirements.

- **Integration:** Check if the system can integrate with your website and other platforms you use. Seamless integration is key to a smooth reservation process.

- **Training:** Ensure that the system provider offers adequate training and support for you and your staff. Proper training ensures everyone can make the most of the system's capabilities.

- **Customization:** Look for a system that allows customization to match your branding and restaurant's unique needs.

- **Data Security:** Verify that the system complies with data security regulations to protect your business and customers' information.

By implementing a reservation system that suits your restaurant's needs, you'll be taking the first step toward efficient Reservation Management. It's a tool that simplifies booking and empowers you with insights to optimize your operations and enhance the guest experience.

Implement Clear Reservation Policies

Now, let's dive into one of the not-so-fun aspects of Reservation Management – crafting clear Reservation Policies.

Why do reservation policies matter?

They set clear expectations and play an important role in ensuring a smooth reservation process, managing guest satisfaction, and avoiding mishaps.

Imagine a scenario where a guest makes a reservation for a party of ten on a busy Saturday night and shows up with only two people. This can disrupt your seating arrangements and potentially lead to empty tables, lost revenue, and disgruntled customers.

Clear reservation policies can help prevent frustrating situations like this.

Here are some suggestions on how to go about it.

- **Cancellation Policy:** Clearly define your cancellation policy, including the required notice period. For example, you might require a minimum of 24 hours notice for cancellations. Your cancellation policy should strike a balance between guest convenience and protecting your business from last-minute cancellations or no-shows.

- **No-Show Policy:** Specify how you handle no-shows. Some restaurants charge a fee for no-shows to deter this behavior and compensate for lost revenue.

PRO TIP: Carefully weigh the pros and cons of charging a fee for no-shows. This might be fine if your restaurant is thriving and booked solid on weekends. However, if your restaurant is new or struggling to get diners, charging a fee might not be acceptable to your guests.

- **Reservation Duration:** Communicate the expected duration of reservations. Setting a time limit for each reservation can help manage turnover and avoid overcrowding if you have a busy restaurant. It can also prevent guests from overstaying their welcome during peak hours.

- **Website and Social Media:** Display your policies prominently on your website and social media profiles to inform potential diners.

- **Confirmation Messages:** Include (*or, better yet, include a link to*) a summary of your policies in reservation confirmation messages to remind guests of your expectations.

PRO TIP: There are two aspects to "reservation duration" that I want to clarify here: **(1)** The time that the reservation will be held for (e.g., stating that a 7:30 pm reservation will be held for 20 minutes – otherwise, their table will be offered to another party); and **(2)** The maximum dining time (e.g., each reservation lasts for a maximum of 2 hours).

- **Party Size Limits:** Set limits on the maximum party size you can accommodate for a single reservation. This prevents overcommitment and ensures a better experience for all guests.

- **Deposit Policy:** Consider implementing a deposit policy for larger parties, special accommodations, or special events. This can help safeguard against last-minute cancellations.

PRO TIP: In some cases, having customers pay upfront to ensure a table makes sense. For example, pubs that serve corned beef around St. Patrick's Day might benefit from having customers pay in advance – this way, revenue is gained upfront, and no-shows are naturally discouraged. You also could have a two-tiered payment structure for special events (i.e., $35 early-bird and $55 at the door).

- **Special Requests:** Encourage guests to communicate any special requests or dietary restrictions at the time of booking. This ensures you can prepare accordingly and enhance their experience.

- **Confirmation Process:** Outline your reservation confirmation process, such as sending a confirmation email or SMS text message to guests. This step helps reduce misunderstandings and confirms the booking.

Establishing and communicating these clear reservation policies protects your restaurant and enhances the overall guest experience. In the next subsection, we'll explore another critical aspect of Reservation Management: assessing your restaurant's capacity to ensure smooth operations.

Perform a Capacity Assessment

Capacity assessment begins with a clear understanding of what your restaurant can comfortably accommodate. It's about finding the sweet spot between maximizing revenue and providing a memorable dining experience.

Here are some tips to get started:

- **Determine Your Physical Space:** Measure the physical space available for guests, considering both indoor and outdoor seating if applicable. This establishes your maximum capacity.

- **Consider Table Types:** Different table configurations can accommodate varying party sizes. Assess the types of tables you have and their flexibility in seating arrangements.

- **Account for Waitstaff and Kitchen:** Remember that your staff needs space to move efficiently, and the kitchen has its own limitations. Overcrowding in the front-of-house can lead to chaos in the back-of-house.

- **Evaluate Peak and Off-Peak Hours:** Understand when your restaurant experiences peak and off-peak hours. This knowledge helps you adjust reservation policies and staff scheduling accordingly.

- **Allow for Flexibility:** Don't overcommit. Leave some room for flexibility in your reservations to accommodate walk-ins and last-minute changes.

By conducting this realistic assessment, you'll gain accurate insights into the maximum number of reservations you can comfortably handle while maintaining a high standard of service.

Once you have a clear picture of your restaurant's capacity, the next step is determining the optimal number of reservations to accept. This requires a delicate balance between maximizing revenue and ensuring a smooth dining experience for your guests.

- **Peak vs. Off-Peak:** Consider different reservation limits for peak and off-peak hours. You might accept more reservations during quieter times and fewer during busy rushes.

- **Table Turnover:** Calculate the average time it takes for a table to turn over. This helps you estimate how many reservations you can accommodate during a specific time frame.

"... a healthy [table turnover rate] for most establishments is typically between 1.5 to 2.5 times per meal service ... However, it's important to note that the ideal rate can be influenced by various factors. Fine dining restaurants or establishments that prioritize a relaxed dining experience may have a lower turnover rate, focusing more on providing impeccable service and fostering a leisurely ambiance. On the other hand, fast-casual or quick-service restaurants may aim for a higher turnover rate to accommodate a larger volume of customers." [2]

BlueCart

- **Staffing Levels:** Ensure you have the right number of staff members on hand to handle the reservations you accept. Understaffing can lead to a chaotic experience for both guests and staff.

- **Reservation Software:** If you're using reservation management software, leverage its features to set and adjust reservation limits based on both real-time and trending data.

By conducting this assessment and determining the optimal number of reservations to accept, you'll be better equipped to provide a positive dining experience while maximizing your restaurant's potential revenue.

---

2. BlueCart, *"What is the Ideal Table Turnover Rate?"*, https://www.bluecart.com/blog/what-is-table-turnover#:~:text=Finding%20the%20ideal%20table%20turnover,2.5%20times%20per%20meal%20service.

Communicate Effectively with Guests

Communication is the glue that holds the entire reservation process together. It's about clarity, courtesy, and consideration.

Here's why effective communication with your guests is paramount.

- **Builds Trust:** When guests receive clear and timely communication, they trust your restaurant to deliver on its promises – including a great meal. This trust goes a long way in building a loyal customer base.

- **Prevents Misunderstandings:** Misunderstandings can lead to dissatisfaction. Effective communication helps prevent confusion about reservation policies, wait times, and special requests.

- **Enhances Guest Experience:** A friendly and informative approach enhances the overall guest experience. It makes guests feel valued and attended to.

- **Handles Issues Gracefully:** Sometimes, despite your best efforts, things can go awry. Effective communication allows you to address issues gracefully, turning a potential problem into an opportunity to delight your guests.

In addition to direct verbal communication with guests at your restaurant, communication before and after the dining phase is also important.

Here are some sample email and text message templates to help you get started.

Sample Reservation Templates

Confirmation Email

Subject: Your Reservation Confirmation at [Your Restaurant Name]

Dear [Guest's Name],

We're delighted to confirm your reservation at [Your Restaurant Name] for [Reservation Date] at [Reservation Time]. Your table is all set, and we can't wait to host you.

In case you need to reach us or make any changes to your reservation, please feel free to reply to this email or call us at [Restaurant Phone Number].

We look forward to seeing you. Get ready for a wonderful dining experience!

Warm regards,

[Your Name]
[Your Restaurant Name]

Reminder Text Message

Hi [Guest's Name],

Just a friendly reminder about your reservation at [Your Restaurant Name] tomorrow at [Reservation Time].

We're looking forward to serving you. If you need to make any changes, please call us at [Restaurant Phone Number].

See you soon!

Warmly,

[Your Restaurant Name]

Follow-up Message (Sent 1 Day After Guest's Visit)

Subject: Thank You for Dining with Us!

Dear [Guest's Name],

We hope you enjoyed your recent visit to [Your Restaurant Name]. It was our pleasure to serve you, and we'd love to hear about your experience.

Please take a moment to share your feedback with us through this [Feedback Survey Link]. Your input helps us continually improve our service.

Thank you for choosing us, and we look forward to hosting you again soon!

Best regards,

[Your Name]
[Your Restaurant Name]

PRO TIP: The reservation confirmation and follow-up messaging should be sent via email AND SMS Text Message. Studies have shown that people are more likely to respond via text message than email, so if possible, ensure that reservation confirmation and feedback requests can be sent via text messages.

Effective communication is an invaluable tool in Reservation Management. It ensures a seamless reservation process and nurtures strong relationships with your guests. In the next subsection, we'll delve into staff training, another critical aspect of reservation success.

Invest in Staff Training

Your staff plays a pivotal role in ensuring a seamless reservation process and a memorable dining experience.

Why?

Because they are the ambassadors of your restaurant. They interact directly with guests, manage seating, and ensure that everything runs as smoothly as possible.

Here are some additional reasons why their role is critical.

- **First Impressions:** Staff members create the first impression of your restaurant. A warm welcome and efficient handling of reservations set the tone for the entire dining experience.

- **Managing Guest Expectations:** Staff should be well-versed in your reservation policies and should communicate them clearly to guests. This prevents misunderstandings and ensures a consistent experience.

- **Efficient Table Management:** Your team needs to know how to manage tables efficiently. This includes seating guests promptly, coordinating with the kitchen, and ensuring a smooth transition between reservations.

- **Flexibility and Problem-Solving:** Staff should be equipped to handle unexpected situations gracefully. This includes managing late arrivals, accommodating special requests, and resolving issues with professionalism and finesse.

Now, let's break down a few key components of staff training that you may want to focus on to improve reservation management:

- **Handling Reservations:** Let's start with the obvious — train your staff on how to handle reservations efficiently. This includes checking the reservation system, confirming bookings, and preparing tables in advance.

- **Managing Walk-Ins:** Your team should be skilled at managing walk-in guests alongside reservations. They need to balance seating availability and ensure fairness in the process.

- **Maintaining a Welcoming Atmosphere:** Staff should create a warm and welcoming atmosphere for all guests. This includes being attentive, responsive, and approachable.

- **Conflict Resolution:** Equip your staff with conflict resolution skills. Sometimes, issues may arise, and your team should be able to address them calmly and professionally.

- **Effective Communication:** Emphasize the importance of clear and effective communication within your team. This ensures that everyone is on the same page and can provide consistent service.

Keep in mind that effective staff training is an investment in your restaurant's success. It enhances the reservation experience while contributing to your restaurant's reputation and long-term success. Staff training will be a recurring theme throughout the book, as all 5 table turnover mistakes will require some element of staff training to remedy.

In the next section, we'll explore the role of data analytics in optimizing your Reservation Management strategy.

Using Data and Analytics to Guide Your Reservation Strategy

In the digital age of dining, having actionable data allows you to make informed decisions and continuously improve your restaurant's operations. Without a doubt, data is your secret weapon in the world of Reservation Management.

Here's why.

- **Data-Driven Decisions:** Analyzing reservation data helps you make informed decisions about everything from seating capacity to staffing levels. This means less guesswork and more strategic planning and coordination with the FOH staff.

- **Demand Forecasting:** Data analytics enable you to forecast demand accurately. You can anticipate peak hours, busy seasons, and even specific days when reservations are likely to surge.

- **Optimizing Reservation Policies:** You can fine-tune your reservation policies by analyzing reservation patterns and guest behavior. For example, you might adjust your cancellation policy based on historical no-show rates.

- **Resource Allocation:** Data can help you allocate resources more efficiently. You'll know when to schedule more staff, increase inventory, or offer promotions to boost reservations during slow periods.

- **Guest Insights:** Analytics can provide valuable insights into guest preferences, allowing you to tailor your offerings and services to meet shifting expectations.

To get started, ensure that your reservation management platform provides detailed analytics on reservation trends, no-show rates, and guest demographics.

In addition to simply collecting data, it is important to review the data periodically.

Here's a 5-step approach that you can implement:

- **Step 1 — Set Review Periods:** Schedule regular intervals for reviewing reservation data. Depending on your restaurant's needs, this could be weekly, monthly, or seasonally.

- **Step 2 — Identify Trends:** Look for patterns in your reservation data. Are there recurring trends in terms of peak hours, popular dishes, promotions, or reservation sources?

- **Step 3 — Evaluate Performance:** Assess how well your reservation management strategies are performing. Are you hitting your target occupancy rates, or are there areas for improvement?

- **Step 4 — Analyze Guest Feedback:** Pay attention to reservation feedback. Do guests mention issues like wait times, booking difficulties, or miscommunications?

- **Step 5 — Adjust Strategies:** Based on your findings, adjust your reservation policies, staff scheduling, and communication strategies to address any identified weaknesses.

By harnessing data analytics and regularly reviewing reservation data, you'll be better equipped to refine your reservation management strategies, enhance guest experiences, and maximize your restaurant's potential.

In the next section, we'll explore why collecting guest feedback is critical to improving your reservation process.

Collect and Utilize Customer Feedback

Listening to your customers is like having a compass that guides you toward continuous improvement. In our final section for this chapter, we'll explore how guest feedback can be a game-changer for your restaurant.

Here's why feedback is a pivotal component of your Reservation Management strategy:

- **Insight into Guest Experience:** Guest feedback provides insights into the real-time experience your guests have with your reservation process and overall dining experience.

- **Identifying Pain Points:** Feedback helps you identify pain points and areas of improvement in your reservation system. This includes pinpointing issues like booking difficulties, long wait times, or miscommunications.

- **Guest-Centric Improvements:** By acting on guest feedback, you can make improvements that matter most to your customers. This not only enhances their experience but also fosters loyalty and positive word-of-mouth.

- **Preventing Repeat Issues:** Regular feedback collection helps you spot recurring issues and address them proactively, preventing similar problems in the future.

- **Competitive Edge:** A restaurant that actively listens to its guests and continually improves is more likely to stand out in a competitive market.

Here are some tips on how to go about collecting and acting on guest feedback:

- **Feedback Collection Points:** Identify key feedback collection points in the reservation process, such as post-dining surveys, online reviews, and direct feedback during the meal.

- **Online Surveys:** Consider sending post-reservation surveys via email and text message, asking guests to rate their experience with the booking process.

- **Engage Actively:** Encourage guests to share their thoughts and experiences through surveys, comment cards, or online review platforms. Make it easy for them to provide feedback.

- **Listen with Empathy:** When you receive feedback, listen with empathy. Understand the guest's perspective, even if the feedback is constructive. Acknowledge their concerns.

PRO TIP: It is natural to take feedback about your restaurant personally. After all, this is your brand, your life's work, and you've poured countless hours into making your restaurant what it is. However, you need to think objectively and, above all, *don't take it personally*.

- **Record and Analyze:** Keep a record of all feedback and analyze it periodically. Look for patterns and common themes that require attention.

- **Act and Improve:** Develop an action plan to address the feedback. Whether it's adjusting reservation policies, improving communication, or enhancing staff training, take tangible steps to make improvements.

- **Follow Up:** After implementing changes, follow up (whenever possible) with guests who provided feedback to let them know you've listened and made improvements based on their input.

- **Express Gratitude:** Always express gratitude to guests who provide feedback, whether it's positive or not. Let them know you value their input and strive for continuous improvement.

By actively collecting and acting on guest feedback, you'll improve your Reservation Management process and foster a culture of excellence that sets your restaurant apart.

In the next section, we'll wrap up this chapter and recap some key takeaways.

Key Takeaways

In this chapter, we explored the critical facets of Reservation Management, dissecting common mistakes that can hinder your success and providing you with actionable strategies to overcome them.

From understanding the consequences of poor reservation handling to implementing reservation management best practices, you've hopefully gained a comprehensive toolkit to elevate your reservation game.

Poor reservation management can lead to overcrowding, frustrated diners, and financial consequences. However, by embracing best practices such as efficient reservation handling, clear reservation policies, capacity assessment, effective communication, staff training, waitlist management, analytics, and feedback collection, you can not only avoid critical mistakes but also transform your restaurant into *"that happy place"* that guests eagerly return to.

As we continue our journey, keep the lessons of this chapter close at hand. Embrace the feedback from your guests, harness the power of data, and strive for continuous improvement. Doing so ensures that every reservation is not just a table booked but a loyal customer in the process.

Let's move on to Mistake #2. See you in the next chapter!

CHAPTER 5
Mistake #2: Slow Service and Kitchen Delays

"It's always imperative to improve and to remain dynamic - or you'll become lunch, as opposed to serving it."

Danny Meyer

Mistake #2 is a challenge that restaurants of all sizes face, but one that can be especially detrimental to new and/or small restaurants where every customer touchpoint matters.

As we discussed, people don't like to wait.

For *anything*.

Especially when they're *hungry*.

They've taken the time to find your restaurant, make a reservation, confirm the reservation, and are looking forward to a delightful meal. As the clock ticks without being served, excitement turns to irritation, and irritation turns to frustration.

Managing a restaurant requires a delicate balance between customer satisfaction and operational efficiency. To do this effectively, you must be able to identify and correct the root cause(s) of slow service and kitchen delays. This isn't just about the ticking of the clock; it's about how time influences the perception of your restaurant in the eyes of your patrons.

Let's start by looking at some of the elements of Mistake #2.

- **Sluggish Service:** Slow service isn't just about the time on the clock. It encompasses the entire front-of-house operation – from the time your customers step through the door to when they finish their meal. It includes how quickly your staff greets and seats guests, takes orders, serves drinks, clears plates, and provides that essential touch of hospitality that defines your establishment. When service is slow, customers inevitably spend more time waiting for their meals and less time enjoying them.

- **Kitchen Delays:** On the flip side, kitchen delays include the time it takes for your chefs to transform orders into dishes and then deliver them to eagerly awaiting diners. This is where the heartbeat of your restaurant's operation is most palpable, as any lag here can send ripples of discontent throughout the entire dining experience.

Many small restaurant owners fail to realize that slow service and kitchen delays are not isolated problems; they're intrinsically connected. A slowdown in service can create kitchen bottlenecks, causing further meal preparation delays. As one exacerbates the other, the dining experience takes a hit, and customers are left waiting longer than they should, growing increasingly impatient. This vicious cycle is a recipe for both customer dissatisfaction and reduced operational efficiency.

This is more than just a time management issue – it's a multifaceted challenge that can mar your restaurant's reputation and impact its profitability. Even more concerning is that this issue tends to grow as your restaurant scales.

Now, let's examine why this critical issue tends to become more visible as sales volume grows.

Impact on Customer Wait Times

Customer wait times lie at the heart of the restaurant industry. They can transform a meal into a memorable experience or a frustrating ordeal. As a small restaurant owner, understanding the intricate relationship between slow service, kitchen delays, and customer wait times is paramount.

> A January 2022 survey analyzed the maximum waiting times people were willing to wait for a table at a restaurant in the United States. While 38% of respondents said they would wait 15 to 30 minutes, 30% would wait 0 to 15 minutes, and just 1% would wait 2 hours or more. [1]
>
> Statista

As mentioned earlier, one of the most tangible and consequential manifestations of Mistake #2 is prolonged customer wait times. As your patrons eagerly await their meals, these moments of anticipation hold the power to shape their entire dining experience.

Indications of Slow Service

---

1. Statista, "Opinions on maximum waiting time for a table at a restaurant in the United States as of January 2022", https://www.statista.com/statistics/1325352/opinions-maximum-waiting-times-at-restaurants-us/#:~:text=A%20January%202022%20survey%20analyzed,stay%20more%20than%20two%20hours.

While you may think that service is progressing at an acceptable rate, it's important to look at things through the eyes of your diners. Slow service is more than just a minor inconvenience; it's a pivotal point where the efficiency of your restaurant begins to suffer.

Slow service manifests in various ways:

- **Ordering Delays:** When your front-of-house staff takes longer to greet and seat customers, capture their orders, or serve drinks, precious minutes tick away. Every delay at this stage directly contributes to the total time a customer spends in your restaurant before even tasting their meal.

- **Course Timing:** As courses progress, slow service becomes even more apparent. Each step - from appetizers to the main course and dessert - can be a potential bottleneck if not managed efficiently. Extended intervals between courses add to the overall wait time.

- **Delayed Check Settlement:** Even after the meal is complete, settling the check should be swift and efficient. Delays in this final step can result in customers spending more time at their tables, affecting table turnover.

The Impact of Slow Service

Now, let's touch on some of the ways slow service impacts the customer experience.

- **Dining Mood:** The mood of your patrons is delicate. Prolonged wait times can affect the overall ambiance of your restaurant. The initial excitement of dining out can dissipate, replaced by frustration or irritability. This can be particularly detrimental to a special occasion or date night.

- **Frustration Mounts:** As minutes turn into extended periods of waiting, frustration can brew. Customers grow restless, wondering why their food hasn't arrived yet. This growing unease can overshadow the entire dining experience, affecting their overall opinion of your restaurant.

- **Expectation vs. Reality:** Every customer enters your restaurant with certain expectations. When prolonged wait times clash with these expectations, it can lead to disappointment. This can overshadow the quality of your cuisine and service, making it harder for your restaurant to earn positive reviews and loyal patrons.

- **Perception of Service:** Prolonged wait times can lead customers to question the efficiency of your service. They might wonder if their orders were lost or forgotten, eroding their confidence in your restaurant's ability to deliver on its promises.

- **Reduced Table Turnover:** Longer wait times directly impact table turnover rates. Which, in turn, directly impacts revenue. When diners linger at their tables for extended periods, it limits the number of customers you can serve in a given time frame, potentially affecting your revenue.

- **Negative Reviews:** In today's interconnected world, dissatisfied customers often turn to online platforms to voice their grievances instead of management. Unfavorable online reviews can deter potential diners and damage your restaurant's reputation.

- **Repeat Business:** The customer experience should never end with a single visit. Satisfied customers are more likely to return and become loyal patrons. Conversely, a negative experience, exacerbated by extended wait times, can deter repeat business and harm your restaurant's long-term prospects.

Recognizing the implications of prolonged customer wait times is essential. It underscores the significance of efficiently managing the service flow, streamlining kitchen operations, and ensuring that your customers receive their meals promptly. Now, let's take a quick look at the impact of kitchen delays.

The Impact of Kitchen Delays

Kitchen delays are the second half of the customer wait time equation. Here's a quick overview of the impact that kitchen delays can have on your overall operation:

- **Order Accuracy:** Rushed or overwhelmed kitchen staff may inadvertently make mistakes, necessitating re-preparing dishes. This not only results in customer frustration but also increases wait times.

- **Order Processing:** Once orders are placed, the journey to the heart of your restaurant – the kitchen – begins. Delays here, caused by a multitude of factors such as under-staffing, inefficiencies, or even the complexity of dishes, can compound the time it takes for a meal to reach the table.

- **Cooking Times:** Certain dishes may require longer preparation, especially if they involve intricate cooking techniques or specialized ingredients. These additional cooking times, while often necessary, can extend the overall wait time for customers.

Now, let's connect the dots. Slow service and kitchen delays are intrinsically intertwined. Slow service can lead to kitchen delays as orders bottleneck, and kitchen delays can, in turn, exacerbate the perception of slow service.

The result?

Prolonged wait times can mar the dining experience and affect your restaurant's reputation.

The Financial Impact

No doubt, this one is near and dear to your heart. Improving overall efficiency isn't just about convenience or customer experience – it's about revenue. The more tables you can serve during peak hours, the greater your revenue potential. Extended wait times jeopardize this potential, thereby directly impacting your bottom line.

As your restaurant's popularity grows, so do the financial implications of slow service and kitchen delays:

- **Higher Staffing Costs:** Extended wait times often require longer shifts for your staff. This can inflate labor costs, eroding your profit margins. Efficient table turnover can help you optimize staffing schedules, aligning labor costs with actual demand.

- **Peak Hour Profitability:** Peak hours are those golden moments when demand peaks and diners are willing to pay a premium for your dishes. Inefficient table turnover during these critical periods dilutes your restaurant's profit potential. Efficiently managing these high-demand windows is essential for maximizing revenue.

- **Missed Revenue:** Every occupied table represents a revenue opportunity. When tables remain occupied for extended periods due to slow turnover rates, service lags, and kitchen delays, it directly impacts your restaurant's daily income. This means that you're missing out on potential sales.

- **Competitive Edge:** In today's competitive restaurant industry, efficient table turnover can provide a crucial edge. A reputation for swift service can attract more customers, enhancing your restaurant's financial stability.

 **PRO TIP:** You should NEVER think of the customer relationship ending with a single visit. The key to long-term profitability is to *think* long-term. You want customers that keep coming back. An unsatisfied customer won't be a loyal customer – meaning that you are potentially missing out on income for years.

Reduced table turnover doesn't merely affect one aspect of your restaurant's finances; it influences multiple facets, from revenue generation to cost management and even your competitive position. The goal is not just serving great food; it's to unlock the full financial potential of your restaurant.

Now, let's look at some best practices for improvement.

Service Efficiency Best Practices

Now that we've looked at some of the critical mistakes, it's time to take proactive steps toward enhancing your restaurant's service efficiency. One of the cornerstones of success lies in streamlining service processes.

Key Focus Areas

In this section, we'll examine some strategies designed to optimize front-of-house (FOH) operations, ensuring that service flows with precision.

- **Efficient Front-Of-House Staffing:** The heartbeat of your restaurant is your staff. Ensuring you have the right number of employees during peak hours is vital. Overstaffing can lead to higher labor costs, while understaffing can result in slower service. Achieving the right balance is key.

- **Table Assignment Strategies:** Implementing effective table assignment strategies can significantly impact service efficiency. Consider factors like server zones, table rotation, and the size of parties to optimize the distribution of guests among your staff.

- **Ordering and Communication Tools:** Investing in modern technology can streamline the ordering process. Handheld devices for servers, digital order-taking systems, and communication tools like headsets can reduce errors and save valuable time – especially in high-volume restaurants or during peak times.

- **Clear Menu Design:** This one's a biggie (*we'll explore this more in a future chapter*). A well-designed menu can expedite the ordering process, but few restaurant owners realize this. Ensure that your menu is easy to read, well-organized, and free from unnecessary "*cheffy*" jargon. Clear menus help customers make choices quickly, reducing wait times.

- **Training and Standardization:** Consistency is the hallmark of efficient service. Thoroughly train your staff to follow standardized procedures, from taking orders to delivering meals. This minimizes confusion and ensures smooth service.

- **Guest Feedback Loop:** Create a feedback loop where guests can express their concerns and provide suggestions. Listening to customer feedback can help you identify service bottlenecks and make necessary improvements.

Streamlining your service flow is a continuous journey toward enhanced efficiency. By fine-tuning these aspects of your restaurant's operations, you pave the way for a dining experience where service is seamless, wait times are minimized, and customers leave with smiles on their faces.

Now, let's dive a bit deeper into some specifics of both service and kitchen efficiency.

More on FOH Service Efficiency

The first step toward efficiency begins with your front-of-house service processes. The goal here is to ensure that every aspect of service flows seamlessly from the moment guests walk through your doors.

Carefully Analyze Your Staffing Efficiency

Adequately staff and prepare for peak hours. Analyze historical data to schedule staff properly during peak hours, special promotions, holidays, events, and large parties. Make sure you have the right number of servers to meet demand without overstaffing.

Cross-train your staff to boost coverage. Consider Cross-training your staff to perform various roles. This flexibility enables you to deploy them where they are needed most, optimizing your service efficiency.

Review Your Table Assignment Strategies

"Play the Zones" Effectively. Divide your restaurant into server zones to optimize table assignments. This allows servers to focus on specific sections, improving their ability to provide timely service.

Consider your Rotation. Be sure to implement a fair table rotation system to ensure that no server is consistently burdened with back-to-back large parties.

Think about Party Size. Consider the size of the party when assigning tables to servers. Of course, smaller parties may require less attention, allowing servers to handle multiple tables.

Embrace Modern Tools and Technology

Invest in Your Order System. Invest in digital order-taking systems to reduce errors and expedite the ordering process.

Use Handheld Devices. Consider equipping servers with handheld devices for orders and payments, allowing them to spend more time on the floor. More visibility and access means faster turnaround times. Likewise, apps can help facilitate quick communication among staff. This can help coordinate service efficiently.

Optimize Your Menu. Read, then re-read your menu. Ensure that it's easy to understand, avoiding both boredom and unnecessary complexity. Convene a focus group if necessary. A clear and concise menu helps customers make choices swiftly, reducing wait times.

Embrace Training and Feedback Loops

Include a Comprehensive Training Program. Thoroughly train your staff on standardized procedures for order-taking, serving, and customer interactions.

Encourage Feedback. Create avenues for guests to provide feedback on their dining experience. Listen to their suggestions and concerns to identify areas for improvement in your service.

An efficient front-of-house operation is a continual journey of optimization. These insights and practical tips can serve as a starting point, guiding you toward a service that's not only swift but also ensures every guest's experience is enhanced. Let's move on to kitchen operations.

More on BOH Kitchen Efficiency

The flow of the kitchen is another crucial aspect of overcoming slow service.

Here are some areas to focus on.

Analyze Your Workflow

Observation: Begin by observing your kitchen during peak hours. Identify areas where congestion or delays occur. Look for patterns and potential choke points.

Layout Optimization: Next, analyze your kitchen's layout. Ensure that workstations are logically arranged, minimizing the distance and time required for chefs and kitchen staff to access ingredients and equipment. Make sure each area is organized for efficient movement and minimal interruptions.

Process Mapping: Create a process map of your kitchen operations. This visual representation can highlight bottlenecks and inefficiencies.

Streamline Processes: Finally, standardize and streamline cooking processes to reduce unnecessary steps. Each additional trip or excess movement in the kitchen can lead to delays.

Equipment Assessment: Regularly assess the condition and performance of your kitchen equipment. Outdated or malfunctioning appliances can slow down food preparation. Regularly communicate with kitchen staff to find out if maintenance or service is needed for any equipment.

Clear Communication Flow

Order Management Systems: Invest in order management systems that facilitate clear communication between the front-of-house and the kitchen. This reduces errors and ensures that orders are prepared promptly.

Implement Kitchen Display Systems: Consider implementing Kitchen Display Systems (KDS). KDS screens can replace paper tickets, allowing chefs to see orders as they come in and prioritize them accordingly. This improves order flow.

Inventory Management

Just-in-Time Inventory: Adopt a just-in-time inventory management system to minimize storage needs and ensure that ingredients are fresh. Reducing excess inventory can minimize ingredient waste, free up space, and reduce clutter.

Regular Inventory Audits: Conduct regular audits to identify slow-moving ingredients and eliminate items that aren't contributing to your menu. This can further optimize storage space.

Supplier Collaboration: Work closely with suppliers to ensure timely deliveries of fresh ingredients. Reliable suppliers can help prevent shortages. If possible, consider local, sustainable producers.

Kitchen Staff Training

Cross-Training. Just like FOH staff, cross-train kitchen staff to handle various tasks. This flexibility can help during busy periods and prevent bottlenecks caused by staff shortages, lack of one or more specific skillsets, or other unforeseen issues that inevitably seem to creep up.

Flexible Staffing. Have a flexible staffing plan to accommodate fluctuations in demand. Review the data, and be ready to bring in additional staff during busy periods.

Time Management. Train your kitchen team in time management techniques to ensure that they work efficiently and maintain a steady pace.

Leverage Technology

Cooking Equipment. Consider investing in modern cooking equipment that offers speed and consistency. High-speed ovens and advanced appliances can reduce cooking times significantly.

Inventory Software. Use inventory management software to track ingredients, reorder supplies automatically, and reduce the risk of running out of essential items.

By implementing these strategies, you'll equip your kitchen to overcome bottlenecks swiftly and help ensure that food preparation is running at an optimal level. A kitchen that operates with minimal interruptions is not only efficient but also capable of consistently delivering great meals to your diners.

Training is the Key to Efficiency

The importance of having an efficient and collaborative staff cannot be understated. They are the real heart and soul of your restaurant, and their skills and abilities help carry your vision to fruition. Training them to work together with precision and harmony is paramount in avoiding service delays.

Let's start with the obvious.

Training your staff to work efficiently means they can navigate their roles swiftly and with precision. This efficiency extends to order-taking, food preparation, and serving. Also, A well-trained team is less prone to errors. Fewer mistakes mean fewer disruptions in service and happier customers.

Customer satisfaction is another reason to invest in staff training. A well-trained team ensures timely service, which directly impacts customer satisfaction. On the other hand, delays can lead to dissatisfaction and lost business. Customers notice and appreciate a seamless dining experience. Properly trained staff contribute to this ambiance.

Comprehensive Onboarding and Training

Structured Training Program(s). Develop structured onboarding programs for new hires. These programs should cover everything from restaurant policies to job-specific responsibilities.

Mentorship. Pair new employees with experienced mentors. This mentorship not only accelerates learning but also instills your restaurant's culture and values.

Role-Specific Training. Tailor your training program to each job role. Servers, chefs, bartenders, and hosts all have unique responsibilities, and their in-house training should reflect that.

Hands-On Experience. Provide hands-on experience and shadowing opportunities. Learning by doing is a powerful way to build skills and confidence.

Customer Service Training

Effective Communication. Train your staff in effective communication skills. Empathy, active listening, and conflict resolution are essential components of exceptional customer service.

Handling Difficult Situations. Prepare your team to handle challenging customer interactions gracefully. Training in de-escalation techniques can be invaluable.

Conflict Management. Equip your staff with conflict resolution skills. In times of stress, the ability to handle conflicts calmly and professionally is invaluable.

Efficiency Under Pressure. Trained employees can maintain their efficiency even during peak hours. They adapt and thrive under pressure rather than succumbing to chaos.

PRO TIP: Many online training platforms offer courses that cover soft skills. Look into platforms like Udemy, LinkedIn Learning, and others. Many times you can find the courses you need under $50 USD (as of the time of writing). The best thing is that once purchased, you own them and they can be re-used for training new staff, or as a refresher course periodically.

Food Safety and Hygiene

Food Safety Training. Ensure that all staff members are thoroughly trained and certified in food safety and hygiene. Compliance with health regulations is paramount.

Regular Refreshers. Conduct regular refresher courses to keep food safety practices top of mind.

PRO TIP: Building a comprehensive training program may seem like a lot, but remember that the reputation of your restaurant is at stake. Poorly trained staff is a big turnoff to customers – especially if you're running a restaurant that caters to high-income patrons. Nobody wants to drop several hundred dollars for a meal when they've received lackluster service.

Investing in employee training not only enhances the skills and competence of your team but also contributes to a harmonious work environment where staff members feel valued and motivated. This, in turn, reflects on the quality of service and the overall dining experience your restaurant offers.

Technology Solutions to Boost Efficiency

Technology solutions can streamline operations, enhance customer experiences, and boost your restaurant's efficiency. Let's discover how these powerful tools can be your ally in avoiding critical service delays.

Point-of-Sale (POS) Systems

Efficient Order Management. Modern POS systems aren't just credit-card machines – they are the backbone of a streamlined order management process. They allow your staff to take orders swiftly and accurately, reducing the risk of errors.

Tableside Ordering. With tableside ordering capabilities, servers can take orders directly at the table, sending them instantly to the kitchen. This not only saves time but also enhances the overall dining experience.

Real-time Updates. POS systems provide real-time updates on table statuses, allowing for quicker turnarounds. Servers can identify available tables promptly, minimizing wait times for guests.

Kitchen Management Software

Efficient Order Prioritization. As mentioned earlier, kitchen management software, such as Kitchen Display Systems (KDS), ensures that orders are prioritized effectively. Chefs can see incoming orders, reducing confusion and delays.

Reduced Paper Clutter. By eliminating paper tickets, KDS systems reduce clutter in the kitchen, making it easier for chefs to focus on cooking.

Inventory Tracking. Some kitchen management software solutions include inventory tracking features. This helps in optimizing ingredient usage and reducing waste, contributing to cost-efficiency.

Digital Inventory Management: Ensuring Ingredient Availability

Automated Reordering. Running out of key ingredients is embarrassing for your staff, slows the order process, and results in a poor customer experience. Inventory management software can automate the reordering of ingredients, preventing shortages.

This ensures that your kitchen always has the necessary supplies to fulfill orders efficiently. Likewise, by tracking ingredient usage and minimizing waste, digital inventory management helps optimize costs while ensuring consistent service.

As we dive deeper into the technological landscape of restaurant management, remember that these tools are not just cool gadgets; they are the gears that keep your restaurant running efficiently.

Technology not only reduces service delays but also enhances the overall dining experience.

Let's move on to our final area – menu optimization.

Menu Optimization for Service Efficiency

Menu optimization is the art of crafting a menu that not only draws in diners but also contributes to service efficiency. While we'll explore this topic in much greater detail in a later chapter, let's touch on how menu optimization can enhance your restaurant's efficiency.

Managing Complexity

Variety vs. Complexity. A well-designed menu strikes the right balance between offering a variety of dishes and managing the complexity of kitchen operations. Too much variety can overwhelm your kitchen staff, leading to kitchen delays.

Ingredient Overlap. Consider how ingredients overlap between dishes. Efficient menu planning minimizes the number of unique ingredients required. Remember that each dish on your menu has a unique preparation time. Balancing these times ensures a smoother workflow in the kitchen.

Peak Hours. During busy hours, your kitchen should be equipped to handle the demand without compromising on food quality. A well-balanced menu supports this.

Allergen and Dietary Information

Transparency. A surprising percentage of diners have food allergies and look for this information on the menu *first*. Including clear allergen and dietary information on the menu saves time while showing consideration for customer needs. Also, make sure that your staff is trained to ask for any allergy sensitivities *up front*. This is especially important if small children also dine at your restaurant.

Kitchen Preparedness. Knowing dietary restrictions in advance allows your kitchen to prepare dishes efficiently and accurately. It also reduces the likelihood of custom orders or last-minute modifications.

Highlighting Menu Focus Areas

Signature Dishes. Spotlighting signature dishes can guide diners toward options that align with your kitchen's efficiency. This helps maintain consistent service.

User-friendly Layout. The menu layout itself can influence ordering efficiency. A well-organized menu can guide diners toward easier-to-prep items.

While menu optimization is a vast and multifaceted topic, it's essential to understand its pivotal role in enhancing service efficiency. In a later chapter, we'll go deeper into the art and science of menu optimization, exploring strategies to refine your menu for operational excellence.

Key Takeaways

We covered a lot of information in this chapter. But efficiency is a pivotal topic that must be covered thoroughly. Remember, the journey toward efficient table turnover is not a one-time sprint but a continuous marathon.

Getting it right requires a deep understanding of your restaurant's unique dynamics, a commitment to excellence in service, and a willingness to adapt to the evolving landscape of technology and customer expectations.

As you move forward, keep these key takeaways in mind.

- **Understand the Problem:** Recognize that slow service and kitchen delays can have a cascading effect on your restaurant's success, especially as sales volume increases.

- **Impact on Customer Wait Times:** Prolonged customer wait times can lead to reduced table turnover efficiency and affect the overall dining experience.

- **Service Efficiency Strategies:** Implement a range of strategies, from streamlining service processes to embracing technology, to prevent slow service and kitchen delays.

- **Financial Implications:** Understand the financial consequences of reduced table turnover and how it can affect your restaurant's bottom line.

- **Menu Optimization:** Consider the significance of a well-designed menu that balances variety and kitchen capacity. We'll explore this topic in greater depth later on.

As we continue our journey, remember that the pursuit of service efficiency is not just about serving guests quickly; it's about creating memorable dining experiences that keep customers coming back.

Let's move on to mistake #3: Poor Seating Optimization.

CHAPTER 6
Mistake #3: Poor Seating Optimization

"Opportunity is missed by most people because it is dressed in overalls and looks like work."

Thomas Edison

The allocation and layout of tables and chairs may seem like an inconspicuous detail amid the chaos of sizzling kitchens and bustling dining rooms.

Yet, nothing could be further from the truth.

Your seating configuration holds the power to either support or undermine your restaurant.

In this chapter, we get into *"Mistake #3: Poor Seating Optimization,"* a problem that plagues many small restaurant owners. It is a silent saboteur, often ignored, but one that can wield tremendous influence over your bottom line and the dining experience you provide to your guests.

At its essence, this mistake is rooted in a lack of foresight—a failure to recognize that every seat within your restaurant holds the potential for profit. It may seem benign — a simple arrangement of tables and chairs, but within this simplicity lies the power to define the success of your establishment.

Why Seating Optimization is Critical

The allocation and arrangement of seats can make or break your restaurant's success. It's not merely about placing chairs around tables; it's about understanding how each seat can be a valuable asset, a source of revenue, and a contributor to your restaurant's reputation.

Put simply, empty seats represent potential revenue left untapped. Inefficiently managed seating leads to underutilized dining spaces during peak hours, while chaotic seating arrangements can deter potential diners and diminish the overall dining experience.

While some small restaurant owners try to squeeze in as many tables as possible, the focus should be on creating a harmonious dining experience.

Seating optimization goes beyond profit; it directly impacts customer satisfaction and perception. Imagine a guest arriving at your restaurant to find it overflowing with people, tables buzzing with activity—a lively, inviting atmosphere.

This subtly influences their perception of your restaurant's popularity and quality, setting the stage for a memorable dining experience.

On the flip side, a restaurant with empty seats (or a poor layout) can leave customers questioning its appeal. They may perceive it as less popular or vibrant, coloring their perception and influencing their expectations even before they take the first bite.

A well-optimized seating arrangement helps strike the right balance, creating an ambiance that resonates with your brand and enhances customer satisfaction.

The Cost of Underutilized Space

It is helpful to remember that every square foot of your establishment is a precious commodity. Yet, it's common for many restaurant owners to overlook a critical aspect of their overall layout—underutilized space.

When you don't maximize seating space, you're literally leaving money on the table. Empty seats during peak hours represent unrealized profit, an opportunity cost that affects your bottom line. But it's not just about the immediate loss of revenue. The impact also affects your ability to invest in other facets of your restaurant like menu enhancements, staff training, and the quality of the dining experience you provide.

Inefficient seating arrangements can disrupt the dining flow, leading to suboptimal guest experiences. Picture the frustration of a guest who arrives to find your restaurant half-empty but waits for a table because your seating isn't optimized. Their dining experience begins on a sour note, which can cast a shadow over the entire meal.

Poor seating arrangements can also lead to bottlenecks, dead zones, and slower service. These challenges not only hinder the guest experience but can also strain your staff and increase the risk of errors and dissatisfaction among both guests and staff.

A restaurant with visible empty seats can subtly signal that your establishment is less popular than it really is. Perception matters greatly in the world of dining, and a bustling, vibrant atmosphere can attract potential diners. Failure to optimize seating space can also make new diners reluctant to offer word-of-mouth recommendations, causing you to miss out on a broader customer base.

Customer Perception & Dining Psychology

The act of going out to eat is more than just food on a plate. Both flavors and ambiance intertwine to create memorable experiences. Empty seats within your restaurant can significantly influence the perception of your establishment's popularity and quality.

Picture this: In your marketing campaigns, your restaurant boasts exceptional cuisine and impeccable service. Yet, it's not enough for your restaurant to simply be great; it must also *appear great*. In the eyes of your patrons, a bustling atmosphere can be just as appealing as a well-crafted dish. And that, my friend, is where the significance of customer perception comes into play.

Let's dive a bit deeper into the psychology of dining, exploring how the presence of empty seats—or lack thereof—affects the way your restaurant is perceived.

The Popularity Paradox

When guests encounter a restaurant with empty seats during peak hours, it triggers a paradox. They might wonder why this particular establishment isn't buzzing with patrons in a city with plenty of dining options. Subconsciously, they might question its popularity and appeal.

On the other hand, a restaurant filled with diners exudes an aura of desirability. It signals that *"this is the place to be,"* the sought-after experience others have discovered and embraced. This perception can lure more customers, creating a self-fulfilling prophecy of popularity.

Quality by Association

Beyond popularity, customer perception extends to the perceived quality of your restaurant. An empty dining room can inadvertently cause guests to question the true quality of your cuisine and service. They might wonder if there's a reason why others aren't dining there, whether it's subpar food or lackluster service.

In contrast, a vibrant restaurant radiates an air of excellence. It suggests that patrons have chosen your restaurant because they trust your food and service quality. This association between a full house and high quality can further boost your restaurant's reputation. More importantly, it reinforces that their decision to choose your restaurant over the competition was the right one.

The Influence on Decision-Making

The link between empty seats and customer perception is crucial because it directly influences decision-making. Diners are more likely to choose a restaurant that appears popular and of high quality. It's a psychological bias rooted in the desire for a positive dining experience.

As a restaurant owner, you have the power to harness this perception to your advantage. By optimizing your seating space, you can create an environment that enhances the dining experience and shapes the narrative around your restaurant. When this happens, every filled seat becomes a testament to your popularity and a nod to your quality.

Subtle Behavioral Influence

Beyond the initial impression, the atmosphere within a restaurant subtly influences customer behavior. A bustling ambiance can enhance the social aspect of dining, encouraging longer stays and additional orders. When guests feel comfortable and engaged in their surroundings, they are more likely to indulge in a leisurely dining experience, contributing to increased revenue per customer. Conversely, a lackluster atmosphere may lead to unwanted quicker turnover as guests opt for a faster meal to escape the uninspiring environment.

A Boon to Reputation

A bustling atmosphere also plays a pivotal role in shaping your restaurant's reputation. In today's age of social media and online reviews, the perception of a restaurant's popularity is a driving force behind its brand image.

Patrons who experience a lively atmosphere are more likely to share their positive experiences, leading to increased word-of-mouth promotion and positive reviews. Today, a single review can sway potential diners, whereas a bustling atmosphere can serve as a powerful marketing tool.

As we continue, remember that the importance of a bustling atmosphere goes far beyond mere aesthetics. It's about crafting an experience that resonates with your guests, shapes their perceptions, and elevates your restaurant's reputation.

Remember that one of your primary goals is not just to fill seats—it's to craft a perception that draws diners to your establishment and leaves them with an exceptional experience to remember.

Seating Optimization Strategies

In this section, we'll explore the art and science of maximizing your restaurant's seating capacity while ensuring the comfort and satisfaction of every guest. From evaluating your current layout to utilizing technology for smarter table assignments, each strategy is designed to fine-tune your seating arrangements and guest satisfaction.

Assess Your Layout

As we have alluded to, the layout of your dining space plays a pivotal role—affecting not only the flow of service but also the perception and satisfaction of your guests.

Here are some practical tips on evaluating your layout.

- **First, Walk the Path of the Guest:** Begin your evaluation by putting yourself in your guest's shoes. Walk through your restaurant from the entrance to the restroom, experiencing the flow as they would. Pay attention to any bottlenecks, awkward corners, or areas where movement seems restricted. Note how easy or challenging it is for guests and staff to navigate.

- **Seat Yourself:** Take a seat at each table in your restaurant. Consider the view, comfort, and proximity to high-traffic areas. Is there a table near the kitchen entrance that might be noisy? Are some tables too close to restrooms, causing discomfort (i.e., bad odors)? Your personal experience can provide valuable insights.

- **Analyze Traffic Patterns:** Observe the movement of guests and staff during peak hours. Are there congestion points where guests and servers cross paths? Are there tables that seem to be ignored because they're situated in less-trafficked areas? Understanding traffic patterns can help you identify areas for improvement.

- **Review Reservation Data:** Analyze your reservation system data to identify trends. Which tables are consistently booked in advance, and which remain vacant? Are there specific time slots or days when certain tables are in higher demand? This information can also help formulate your seating strategy.

- **Seek Feedback:** Don't hesitate to seek feedback from your staff. Your servers are on the front lines and can provide valuable insights into guest preferences and operational challenges. They may have suggestions for optimizing your seating layout based on their daily experiences.

- **Consider Flexibility:** Think about the flexibility of your seating arrangements. Are your tables fixed in place, or can they be easily moved or rearranged? Flexible seating can allow you to adapt to different group sizes and events, maximizing space utilization.

- **Consult Experts:** If needed, consider consulting restaurant design experts or architects. They can provide professional assessments and recommendations to optimize your layout for both functionality and aesthetics.

Remember, this assessment aims to identify areas for improvement in your restaurant's seating layout. Every detail you uncover is a step toward a better dining experience. By following these tips, you'll be well on your way to fine-tuning your layout and creating a more efficient, guest-centric, and profitable dining space.

Identify Bottlenecks, Dead Zones and Wasted Space

As you continue optimizing your restaurant's seating layout, you'll need to sharpen your observational skills to uncover areas hindering efficiency and guest satisfaction. Let's look at identifying bottlenecks, dead zones, and wasted space—key elements of your layout assessment that can make or break your restaurant's success.

Bottlenecks: Where Flow Stumbles

Bottlenecks in your restaurant's layout can severely disrupt the flow of service and guest movement.

Here are a few practical tips for identifying them.

- **Observe Traffic Congestion:** During peak hours, watch for areas where guests or staff seem to cluster or where movement becomes sluggish. These are likely bottleneck zones.

- **Note Gathering Points:** Pay attention to spots where guests tend to gather while waiting. Are these areas blocking pathways or creating congestion?

- **Consider Server Paths:** Assess whether servers face obstacles or long distances between the kitchen and dining areas. Are there areas where they frequently get stuck, delaying orders?

Dead Zones: Where Potential Income Languishes

Dead zones in your restaurant are areas that rarely see activity or are underutilized. Think of them as the dusty corners of an attic that are often forgotten.

To spot dead zones, look for:

- **Empty Tables and Corners:** Identify tables or corners that are consistently unoccupied during peak hours. These are prime candidates for dead zones.

- **Underused Spaces:** Pay attention to spaces that serve no functional purpose or lack ambiance. Could they be transformed into revenue-generating areas?

- **Evaluate Aesthetics:** Consider whether certain areas lack visual appeal, leading guests to avoid them. Dead zones may actually be design challenges waiting to be addressed.

Let's move on to wasted space.

Wasted Space: Where Opportunities Slip Away

When considering layout optimization, wasted space is the enemy of profitability. It represents areas where potential revenue slips through your fingers.

To pinpoint wasted space, look for:

- **Empty Aisles:** Assess the width of aisles and pathways. Are they unnecessarily wide, consuming valuable square footage?

- **Unused Vertical Space:** Consider whether your restaurant has unused vertical space. Could you add storage, shelving, or hanging décor to free up floor space?

- **Non-Functional Zones:** Identify areas that serve no clear purpose or lack functionality. Every square foot should contribute in some way to guest satisfaction or operational efficiency.

By identifying bottlenecks, dead zones, and wasted space in your restaurant's layout, you're taking the first step toward crafting an optimized seating arrangement that enhances efficiency, guest comfort, and profitability.

Flexible Seating Arrangements

A key step toward optimizing your restaurant's layout is to embrace adaptability and versatility. Let's dive into some of the principles and strategies of flexible seating, enabling you to create a dynamic dining space.

From modular furniture that can be rearranged at will to movable partitions that adapt to different group sizes, the idea behind flexible seating is to empower your restaurant with the agility it needs to thrive.

The Power of Adaptable Seating

Adaptable seating arrangements can transform to suit virtually any occasion, be it an intimate dinner for two, a lively gathering of friends, or a corporate event.

Here are some key benefits:

- **Maximized Seating Capacity:** Adaptable seating allows you to accommodate a wide range of group sizes, from cozy twosomes to larger parties. This means fewer empty tables during peak hours and increased revenue.

- **Enhanced Guest Comfort:** Guests appreciate the flexibility to choose a seating arrangement that suits their preferences. It's about offering options that empower them to tailor their dining experience.

- **Optimized Efficiency:** A restaurant that can swiftly adapt to varying group sizes can seat and serve guests more efficiently. This translates to shorter wait times, quicker table turnovers, and happier guests.

- **Increased Event Opportunities:** With adaptable arrangements, you can cater to private events, from parties to business meetings, without disrupting the regular dining flow. This can open up new revenue streams.

Now, let's see how to do this.

How to Implement an Adaptable Seating Plan

Adaptable seating is more than just rearranging tables on a whim. It requires strategic planning and the right tools:

- **Modular Furniture:** Invest in tables and chairs that can be easily moved and reconfigured, allowing you to create various seating arrangements.

- **Movable Partitions:** Use partitions or screens that can be adjusted to create semi-private dining areas or to separate larger groups. These versatile barriers are quick to set up and easy to store, adding an extra layer of adaptability.

- **Stackable Seating:** Consider stackable chairs that can be stored or rearranged as needed. These are particularly useful for optimizing space when large groups require it.

Adaptable seating arrangements support your ability to cater to the needs of your patrons. It's a commitment to versatility, efficiency, and a memorable dining experience.

Okay, let's how your reservation system factors into seating optimization.

The Role of Reservation Systems

Your reservation systems and processes are the key to ensuring that your restaurant is prepared to welcome guests. But without the right tools, things can get chaotic very quickly. That's where reservation systems come into play, helping to harmonize the dining experience.

The Peak Hour Predicament

Peak hours in a restaurant are like the crescendo of a symphony—intense and demanding. Managing seating during this period can be a challenge. This is where a good reservation system proves its worth.

Efficient Seating Allocation: Reservation systems allow you to allocate tables in advance, ensuring that guests are seated promptly upon arrival. This reduces the chaos and minimizes wait times.

Optimal Table Assignments: By considering factors such as table size, guest preferences, and server availability, reservation systems help in making precise table assignments. This contributes to a smoother dining experience.

Managing Guest Expectations: When guests make reservations, they have a clear expectation of when they'll be seated. Reservation systems enable you to meet these expectations, enhancing guest satisfaction.

Data-Driven Insights: Modern reservation systems generally come with analytics tools that provide valuable insights. You can analyze peak hour trends, identify busy periods, and adjust staffing accordingly.

By implementing a reservation system tailored to your restaurant's needs, you're enhancing the efficiency of seating during peak hours and elevating the dining experience.

Balancing Efficient Turnover with Guest Experience

One of the most challenging aspects of table turnover is finding the delicate balance between efficiency and preserving a remarkable dining experience. Achieving efficiency without compromising the quality of the customer experience is a tightrope walk.

Your guests step into your restaurant with expectations that go beyond the food. They anticipate an atmosphere of relaxation, unhurried conversation, and a chance to savor each moment. Pushing for rapid turnovers at the expense of their experience can lead to dissatisfaction and even deter repeat visits.

Here are some strategies to consider:

- **Pacing Courses:** Properly paced courses ensure that guests don't feel rushed. It's about serving each dish at just the right moment, allowing them to savor flavors and enjoy the company.

- **Clear Communication:** Train your staff to communicate empathetically. Let guests know if their table has a time constraint and offer options, such as a drink at the bar while they wait.

- **Seamless Service:** Efficient service doesn't mean hurried service. Ensure that your staff is attentive, knowledgeable, and capable of delivering an exceptional experience, even during busy times.

- **Reservation Timing:** When guests make reservations, encourage them to specify if they have time constraints (especially during lunch hours or for business parties). This information can help you plan accordingly.

- **Utilize Technology:** Reservation systems and table management software can provide real-time data on table availability and wait times, allowing for better planning.

Gently Encouraging Guests to Vacate Tables

Inevitably, there comes a point when the one dining experience must end to make way for the next one. Gently encouraging guests to vacate their tables when necessary requires finesse. It's about creating a seamless transition without making anyone feel hurried or unappreciated.

Here are some ideas to consider:

- **Courteous Communication:** Train your staff to communicate with departing guests courteously and professionally. Let them know that their dining experience is valued and that the next reservation is eagerly anticipated.

- **Offer a Comfortable Waiting Area:** If there's a wait for a table, ensure that your restaurant has a comfortable waiting area. Guests will be more understanding of the need to vacate if they have a pleasant place to continue their conversation.

- **Incentives for Cooperation:** Consider offering incentives for guests who vacate promptly. This could be in the form of a complimentary dessert (to go), encouraging them to leave on a positive note.

- **Efficient Bill Settlement:** Expedite the bill settlement process. Offer the check promptly, and if possible, provide mobile payment options to expedite the process.

- **Use Technology:** Implement a table management system that allows you to monitor the progress of each table. This way, you can anticipate when a table will be ready for the next reservation.

- **Mindful Timing:** Consider the timing of your reservations. Leave a buffer between bookings to allow for a relaxed end to one meal and a smooth beginning for the next.

By implementing these strategies, you optimize table turnover and cultivate a reputation for exceptional service. Guests will appreciate the attention to detail and the effort to make their transition a seamless part of their dining journey.

The Role of Staff Training

Staff training is the cornerstone of consistency, ensuring that every encounter meets your high standards. Hosts and hostesses are the first faces guests encounter, and waitstaff are their guides throughout the dining experience. Their understanding of seating optimization is instrumental in creating a seamless and enjoyable experience for your diners.

Focus on these key elements to ensure your staff excels in this area.

- **Guest Recognition:** if possible, teach your staff to recognize regulars and pay attention to special occasions. This allows for personalized service and helps manage seating preferences.

- **Reservation Management:** Train your team to handle reservations effectively. They should understand how to allocate tables based on reservation times, guest needs, and preferences.

- **Table Awareness:** Each member of your team should be acutely aware of the status of each table and understand when guests are arriving, dining, and departing. Furthermore, they should know when and how to gently encourage guests to vacate their tables when necessary.

- **Communication:** Effective communication is vital. Staff should be highly skilled at conveying wait times, managing expectations, and handling seating-related inquiries.

- **Pacing:** Teach your team how to pace seating to avoid overwhelming the kitchen and ensure a smooth flow of service. Additionally, they should understand the importance of pacing service to align with table turnover goals. Getting this right means that guests are neither rushed nor left waiting.

- **Problem-Solving:** Equip your staff with problem-solving skills. They should be prepared to handle seating challenges, such as accommodating large parties, special requests, unanticipated conflicts, or unexpected walk-ins.

Guided by well-trained staff, efficient seating management sets the tone for an exceptional dining experience. When your hosts and waitstaff understand their vital role in seating optimization, they become key players in the success of your restaurant. They contribute to a harmonious service flow, ensuring every guest enjoys a memorable dining experience.

Handling Seating Concerns and Requests

Exceptional customer service includes addressing concerns and fulfilling guest requests related to seating. When handled properly, it can turn potential obstacles into opportunities to impress your diners.

Here are some practical tips:

- **Practice Active Listening:** Train your staff to actively listen to guest concerns and requests. They should empathize and respond promptly. Additionally, they should be trained in conflict-resolution skills so that they can handle challenging situations diplomatically and professionally.

- **Flexible Seating:** Whenever possible, accommodate seating preferences and requests. Whether it's a quiet corner, a window view, or proximity to the bar, fulfilling these requests can enhance guest satisfaction.

- **Special Occasions:** Be prepared to handle special occasions gracefully. Anniversaries, birthdays, and marriage proposals are opportunities to make the dining experience truly memorable.

Remember, these events are often highly shared on social media platforms, giving you an opportunity to capitalize on free publicity.

Handling customer concerns and requests related to seating is an art that can transform moments of potential discomfort into showcases of exceptional service. When guests feel heard and valued, they are more likely to become loyal patrons and ambassadors for your restaurant.

Comfort and Accessibility

Let's look at an often-overlooked aspect of seating optimization – the importance of comfort and accessibility. Your restaurant must provide not only comfortable seating for guests to fully savor the dining experience but also feature accessibility to ensure that everyone, regardless of their mobility or special needs, can enjoy their meal.

Here are some strategies for ensuring comfort and accessibility:

- **Ergonomic Design:** Invest in ergonomic furniture that supports good posture and comfort. Well-designed chairs and tables can enhance the dining experience.

- **Adequate Space:** Ensure that there's enough space between tables to accommodate wheelchairs and provide easy navigation for all guests.

- **Accessible Facilities:** Make sure your restaurant has accessible restrooms and ramps for guests with mobility challenges. Compliance with accessibility standards is essential and a sign of inclusivity.

- **Flexible Seating:** Offer seating options that cater to various preferences, including booth seating for privacy and communal tables for social interactions.

**PRO TIP:** The sobering truth is that we (Americans) are getting fatter. I know that's not politically correct to say, but it is a fact. According to one source, *"Twenty-two states had an adult obesity rate at or above 35%... and every U.S. state had an obesity rate of at least 20%"*[1] It is important to factor in the growing waistlines of guests when choosing furniture and seating layouts.

- **Regular Maintenance:** Periodically inspect and maintain your furniture to ensure it remains comfortable and in good condition.

Closely coupled with comfort is accessibility. Adhering to accessibility standards isn't just about legal requirements; it's about creating an environment where everyone feels welcome and valued.

Here are some tips for Adhering to Accessibility Standards:

- **Research ADA Compliance:** Familiarize yourself with the Americans with Disabilities Act (ADA) guidelines for restaurants. Ensure your restaurant fully complies with accessibility features such as ramps, accessible restrooms, and designated parking spaces.

**PRO TIP:** As with anything related to legal compliance, talk to a lawyer. Getting slapped with an ADA lawsuit is both costly and embarrassing and can quickly turn into a PR nightmare.

---

1. VOA, *"America Keeps Getting Fatter — These Are the Heaviest States of All"*. Link: https://www.voanews.com/a/7312757.html

- **Provide Accessible Menus:** Provide accessible menus for guests with visual impairments, including Braille or digital menu options that can be accessed via smartphones or other devices. When updating your menu, don't forget to update accessible menus as well.

- **Training:** Train your staff to be knowledgeable about accessibility features and to assist guests with disabilities as needed. Sensitivity and awareness can go a long way in creating an inclusive environment.

- **Feedback Mechanism:** Establish a feedback mechanism for guests to report any accessibility issues they encounter. This proactive approach allows you to address concerns promptly and helps prevent these concerns from being voiced online.

- **Regular Audits:** Periodically audit your restaurant's accessibility features to ensure they remain functional and in compliance with current standards.

Adhering to accessibility standards and guidelines isn't just a legal requirement; it's a commitment to offering an exceptional dining experience for every guest. By making your restaurant welcoming and accessible, you ensure that all patrons can enjoy their meals.

Data-Driven Seating Optimization

Successful seating optimization depends on the ability to read and understand the diners in your establishment. While personal experience and intuition are important, they cannot substitute for tangible data. Data remains even after your guests leave, so harnessing analytics and monitoring to refine your restaurant's seating optimization is critical.

Here are some strategies for leveraging data and analytics to optimize seating:

- **Guest Behavior Analysis:** Dive into the data to understand when your restaurant is busiest, which tables are most popular, and how long guests typically linger. Use this insight to optimize table assignments and pacing.

- **Reservation Trends:** Analyze reservation data to predict peak hours and plan accordingly. Adjust staffing levels and seating arrangements to match expected demand.

- **Menu Performance:** Track which menu items have longer prep times and cross-reference their ordering process with the data from table turnovers. Consider offering quick-to-prepare options during busy periods.

- **Customer Feedback:** Use feedback and reviews to identify areas for enhancing seating optimization. Address concerns promptly and make improvements based on customer input.

- **Competitive Benchmarking:** Compare your restaurant's performance with competitors. Identify strengths and weaknesses in seating optimization and learn from emerging trends and industry leaders.

Insights gained from data and analytics will help you enhance table turnover and set the stage for a dining experience that leaves guests wanting more.

Leverage Metrics

Data doesn't exist in a vacuum. Knowing which data to focus on is even more important than simply collecting data. This is where metrics come into play. You must understand which key metrics to focus on to enhance table turnover and seating efficiency.

Metrics are like an X-ray of your restaurant, offering insights into how well your seating optimization strategies are performing. By tracking metrics, you can not only measure your restaurant's efficiency but also identify areas for improvement and make data-driven decisions that lead to higher profits and happier guests.

Here are some key metrics to focus on for seating optimization:

- **Table Turnover Rate:** Calculate how quickly tables are being occupied and vacated. A higher turnover rate indicates greater efficiency.

- **Occupancy Rate:** Measure the percentage of time your tables are occupied during operating hours. An optimal occupancy rate maximizes revenue.

- **Reservation No-show Rate:** Track how often guests with reservations fail to show up. This metric helps you manage reservations more effectively.

- **Seating Capacity Utilization:** Analyze how effectively you're utilizing your restaurant's seating capacity. Identify underutilized areas or time slots.

Data without analysis is useless. Regularly review and analyze these metrics to uncover trends and patterns. Use this information to adjust your seating optimization strategies, staffing levels, and reservation policies for maximum efficiency.

Key Takeaways

Seating optimization isn't simply a matter of arranging tables and chairs; it's a pivotal element that influences every aspect of your restaurant's operations. Efficient seating directly impacts your table turnover rate—the lifeblood of profitability in the restaurant industry. Ensuring guests are seated promptly and comfortably maximizes your revenue potential and greatly improves the dining experience.

Here are a few Key Takeaways:

- **Efficiency Equals Profitability:** Seating optimization is not just about filling chairs; it's about maximizing revenue and creating a positive guest experience.

- **Data-Driven Decision-Making:** Embrace the world of data and analytics. Invest in technology that tracks and analyzes key metrics, enabling you to fine-tune your seating strategies for maximum efficiency.

- **Continuous Improvement:** Successful restaurants never stop fine-tuning their seating operations. Be adaptable and open to change.

- **Guest-Centric Approach:** Keep your guests at the center of your strategies, ensuring their comfort and satisfaction.

- **Strive for Balance:** Achieving the right balance between efficient turnover and a pleasant dining experience is the hallmark of a well-managed restaurant.

- **Staff Training:** Equip your team with the knowledge and skills to manage seating efficiently. Ensure hosts and waitstaff understand their critical role in the guest experience.

One final note. Remember that you are not alone in this journey. The restaurant community is filled with resources, associations, and experts who can guide you along the way. Seek advice, network, and learn from others who have successfully mastered the art of seating optimization.

Okay, let's move on to Mistake #4: Poor Waitlist Management.

CHAPTER 7
Mistake #4: Poor Waitlist Management

"Men are rich only as they give. He who gives great service gets great rewards."

Elbert Hubbard, Artist and Writer

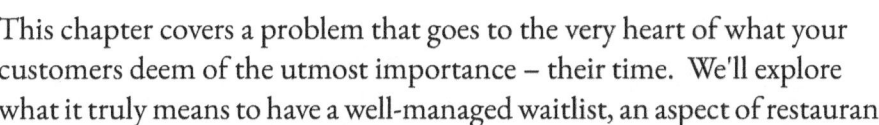

This chapter covers a problem that goes to the very heart of what your customers deem of the utmost importance – their time. We'll explore what it truly means to have a well-managed waitlist, an aspect of restaurant operation that extends far beyond jotting down names and approximate wait times. Poorly handled, it can lead to frustrated patrons, overburdened staff, and revenue slipping through the cracks.

As we navigate through the challenges and opportunities that come with waitlist management, you'll gain insights into the modern influences and shifting expectations that have reshaped the dining landscape – especially post-COVID. From the pervasive influence of social media to the emergence of one-day delivery services, we'll uncover the forces at play that make proficient waitlist management more imperative than ever.

Understanding Waitlist Management

Let's take a step back and set the stage for our discussion by defining what a waitlist truly is. At its core, a waitlist is more than just a ledger or a list of names. It regulates the flow of patrons, ensuring that tables are occupied efficiently and diners are seated fairly.

Beyond its functional role, a waitlist is a promise. It is a commitment to your customers that their presence is valued, their wait will be respected, and their dining experience will be handled with care. It is a silent agreement, setting expectations and forming the initial perception of your establishment.

Poor waitlist management is often characterized by the following.

- **Disorganization:** A poorly managed waitlist is a breeding ground for chaos. If patrons arrive and their names are lost in the shuffle, or they receive inconsistent wait time estimates, you're on a slippery slope to customer dissatisfaction.

- **Neglected Technology:** Technology can be a powerful ally in waitlist management in our modern age. Neglecting solutions like waitlist apps and reservation systems is akin to using a horse-drawn carriage on a superhighway.

- **Underestimating the Impact:** Perhaps the gravest error is underestimating the impact of poor waitlist management. It's not a minor inconvenience; it's a ticking time bomb that can erode customer loyalty, damage your brand, and affect your bottom line.

Today, managing your waitlist is more important than ever. Modern diners have little tolerance for extended wait times, disorganization, or uncertainty in the dining experience.

Let's look at some of the reasons why.

Why Customers Are Unwilling to Wait

Let's start unraveling the profound impact of customer impatience and the modern influences that have reshaped the dining experience.

Going back, say, 20 or even 10 years ago, diners embraced the leisurely pace of a restaurant meal. The mere act of dining out was a respite from the hustle and bustle of daily life. Today, however, the era of instant gratification has ushered in a new set of customer expectations.

Today's diners are accustomed to a world where information (and everything else) is at their fingertips. Goods arrive within a day's notice, and entertainment is instantaneously streamed. Once considered a virtue, patience is now all but extinct in society.

Customer impatience, while challenging, is not totally without reason. It stems from a life where time is a precious commodity. Long wait times or inefficient service can quickly turn eager anticipation into frustration.

You simply cannot afford to make customers wait for an extended period of time to be seated – especially when they're hungry.

Here are some of the modern influences that have exacerbated customer impatience.

- **Social Media:** The realm of dining has become intertwined with social media, where customers share their culinary adventures via "selfies" and "instant reels." A single negative experience can be broadcast to a large audience in real-time, causing reputational damage that can be difficult to repair. Worse yet, even if the staff resolves the problem, there is no guarantee that a positive resolution will be shared. Audiences prefer bad news over good news.

- **One-Day Delivery Times:** The rise of e-commerce giants like Amazon has set a new standard for speedy service. The promise of one-day delivery has subconsciously conditioned consumers to expect rapid results, even in the realm of dining.

- **Delivery Platforms:** Customers now have the choice of having food delivered to their homes at a fraction of the time it takes to travel to your restaurant, be seated, and enjoy a meal. The rise of "Ghost Kitchens" (virtual restaurants that have no physical location and only operate on delivery platforms) adds further competition to traditional restaurant models.

- **Instant Content:** The digital age has created a culture of instant gratification. People can access vast content and information at the touch of a screen or the click of a button. This culture extends to dining, where patrons expect prompt service and immediate satisfaction.

Now, let's look at some of the consequences of poor waitlist management.

Consequences of Poor Waitlist Management

If not addressed, poor waitlist management has far-reaching implications. This can send shockwaves through your entire restaurant operation. At its core, it's a failure to orchestrate the flow of patrons effectively, and this failure can manifest itself in various ways:

- **Frustrated Customers:** Imagine a group of hungry diners arriving at your restaurant, only to be met with confusion and lengthy wait times. Their patience wears thin, and hunger turns to irritation. Frustrated customers are unlikely to return and often share their negative experiences with others.

- **Overburdened Staff:** Poorly managed waitlists burden your staff with the impossible task of juggling a multitude of factors - walk-ins, reservations, table turnovers, and customer expectations. This creates operational chaos and leads to stressed and demotivated employees.

- **Financial Repercussions:** When tables remain vacant due to mismanagement, your restaurant loses revenue. The financial impact of poor waitlist management is real, and it can eat into your profits.

- **Tarnished Reputation:** In the age of online reviews and social media, a single disgruntled customer's experience can have a ripple effect. Negative reviews can spread like wildfire, and your restaurant's reputation can be at serious risk before you know it.

Let's take a closer look at how some of these scenarios play out.

How Poor Waitlist Management Frustrates Customers

Okay. Now, let's get to the heart of the matter—how poor waitlist management can be the catalyst for customer frustration.

As minutes turn into a seemingly endless waiting game, your customers' patience wears thin. They grow restless, and their eagerness turns into frustration. Each passing moment becomes a reminder of their precious time at your restaurant instead of doing something else, and their high expectations for the rest of the dining experience begin to fade.

Another common pitfall of poor waitlist management is inconsistent or inaccurate wait time estimates. Imagine telling a party of diners that they'll have to wait for 15 minutes, only to have them twiddling their thumbs for half an hour or more. Discrepancies between expectations and reality are breeding grounds for discontent.

Trust is an invaluable currency. Customers' trust in your establishment erodes when they receive inaccurate information about their wait times, leaving them feeling deceived and dissatisfied.

But it doesn't end there. In the chaos of poor waitlist management, names can get lost in the shuffle, and patrons can be forgotten. Imagine the frustration of a group that's been left languishing in a corner, neglected and overlooked, while others who arrived later are seated promptly. This oversight not only exacerbates frustration but can also lead to a sense of disrespect and disregard.

Finally, the frustration experienced by one party can have a ripple effect. Discontent often tends to spread among diners as they share their grievances with one another.

The result?

An atmosphere charged with negativity that can tarnish the dining experience for everyone in your restaurant.

In this age of instant gratification, customers have grown accustomed to swift service and accurate information. Poor waitlist management disrupts this expectation, leading to customer dissatisfaction and potentially damaging your restaurant's reputation.

Social Media Platforms as an Amplifier

In today's interconnected world, social media has the power to amplify the impact of the dining experience. The dining experience doesn't end when the bill is paid, and the table is cleared. It continues to linger online, where every moment can be shared, scrutinized, and hyped up.

When customers endure chaotic waitlist management, their expectations of a memorable evening are quickly dashed as minutes turn into an eternity of waiting. However, in the modern age of social media, patrons are armed with a powerful tool—their smartphones.

They are able to capture every moment, whether it's the beautifully plated dishes or the frustration etched on their faces as they endure long wait times. These moments can be instantly shared with a vast audience through platforms like Instagram, Facebook, Twitter, and Yelp.

The impact of a single post can be profound. A dissatisfied customer's negative experience, broadcasted to friends, followers, and strangers alike, can set off a chain reaction. The ripple effect of negative reviews and comments can damage your restaurant's reputation in ways that were previously unthinkable.

Before even setting foot in your establishment, potential customers may be influenced by the online remarks of disgruntled customers. A slew of negative reviews or viral posts can deter potential diners, resulting in lost revenue and a tarnished reputation.

On the flip side, effective waitlist management can be a source of positive social media content. Happy patrons who receive timely updates, experience efficient service, and enjoy a seamless dining experience are likely to share their delight online. These positive testimonials can act as a magnet, drawing new customers to your restaurant and enhancing your brand's image.

Throughout this chapter, we'll cover strategies to avoid the negative effects of poor waitlist management and leverage the power of social media to your advantage. By mastering this aspect of restaurant management, you'll be better equipped to ensure that your patrons' experiences are not only satisfying but shareable, further boosting your restaurant's credibility.

Waitlist Management Best Practices

Let's jump into the nitty-gritty details, providing some tools that will streamline your front-of-house operations, including communication, digital notifications, and managing guest expectations.

Communicate with Waiting Customers

In this section, we'll explore the nuances of communication with waiting customers, from the initial greeting to the final farewell. We'll cover some strategies to keep your patrons in the loop, manage their expectations, and ensure that their wait is as pleasant as possible.

It seems simple enough, but many small restaurant owners overlook communicating with diners in the hustle and bustle of service. But one of the most potent tools for effective waitlist management is providing timely updates to waiting customers. As they eagerly await a table, how you keep them informed during this period can significantly influence their perception of your establishment.

Timely communication sets and manages expectations. When patrons are kept in the dark about their wait times or the progress of their reservation, they subconsciously perceive a loss, frustration can brew, and anticipation can quickly turn into impatience.

On the other hand, when they receive an estimated wait time upon arrival and periodic updates thereafter, they gain (or regain) a sense of control and certainty. This makes the wait more bearable and helps build trust between your restaurant and customers.

Modern technology can be a powerful ally in providing timely updates to waiting customers. Today's waitlist management platforms often include text message notifications or pair with apps that inform diners about their table status. These tools enhance efficiency and elevate the overall customer experience.

Yet, while technology plays a crucial role, the human touch should never be underestimated. Your staff's ability to communicate updates with warmth, empathy, and courtesy can turn what might be perceived as an inconvenience into an opportunity to make a positive impression.

By providing your waiting customers with clear and accurate information, you can manage their expectations and create an atmosphere of transparency and trust. When patrons feel well-informed and respected during their wait, they are more likely to leave your restaurant with a positive impression.

Let's pivot to another often-overlooked aspect of customer expectations—your waiting area.

Have an Open, Inviting Waiting Area

Effective waitlist management encompasses the entire waiting period. A well-thought-out and well-designed waiting area not only keeps guests comfortable but also conveys an air of professionalism and consideration.

Consider providing comfortable seating options for waiting guests. Whether it's plush chairs, barstools, or even a cozy bench, the goal is to ensure that patrons are at ease while they wait. Comfortable seating can go a long way in preventing discomfort and restlessness during the waiting period.

A cluttered or disorganized waiting area can lead to confusion and frustration. Make sure that the waiting area is well-marked and easy to navigate. Use clear signage to direct patrons to the correct spot and provide a visible and organized system for tracking their place in line.

The visual aesthetics of the waiting area should align with your restaurant's overall ambiance and brand. A clean, well-maintained space with pleasing decor can enhance the waiting experience and contribute positively to the overall impression of your establishment.

To make the wait more enjoyable, consider offering entertainment options. This could include reading materials, Wi-Fi access, or even a small play area for families with children. The goal is to keep patrons engaged and content while they await their tables.

Displaying information about your restaurant, such as its history, menu highlights, or chef's recommendations, can also be a subtle way to engage waiting patrons and pique their interest – giving the perception of time passing more quickly.

Creating an open and welcoming waiting area is about creating a positive first impression and setting the tone for the rest of the dining experience.

By paying attention to the waiting area's design, comfort, and organization, you can ensure that diners feel valued and well-cared for from the moment they step through your doors.

Managing Guest Expectations

The way that you manage guest expectations can significantly influence a customer's perception of the wait and, ultimately, their satisfaction. Properly managing expectations begins with transparency and honesty. Guests feel informed and in control when they have accurate information about wait times and the dining process. Misleading or purposely underestimating wait times can lead to frustration and disappointment.

One of the most critical aspects of managing expectations is setting realistic wait time estimates. It's better to slightly overestimate and pleasantly surprise guests when their table is ready than to promise a shorter wait and leave them feeling frustrated.

Understanding your restaurant's peak hours and the ebb and flow of customer traffic is also essential. During peak times, wait times may naturally be longer, so it's crucial to communicate this effectively to guests. Additionally, your staff should be prepared to answer questions, provide updates, and ensure that each guest feels valued and understood during their wait.

In the event of unforeseen delays, such as kitchen backlogs or unexpected rushes, it's important to communicate these delays promptly and professionally. Providing explanations and, when possible, compensatory gestures like complimentary appetizers or beverages can go a long way in diffusing frustration.

Managing expectations effectively is not just a simple courtesy but a crucial component of waitlist management. When guests feel that they are informed, valued, and respected during their wait, they are more likely to leave your restaurant with a positive impression, eager to return for another memorable dining experience.

Adopt Digital Notifications Whenever Possible

The adoption of digital notifications has emerged as a powerful way to connect with guests who eagerly wait to be seated. Leveraging these tools properly can significantly enhance their interaction with your restaurant.

Digital notifications, commonly in the form of SMS messages or mobile app alerts, offer a streamlined and efficient means of communication with waiting patrons. These notifications serve as a bridge that keeps guests informed and engaged during their wait.

One of the primary advantages of digital notifications is their speed and accuracy. When a table becomes available, a simple tap of a button can alert waiting guests instantly. This minimizes the chances of misunderstandings and ensures that patrons are notified promptly.

PRO TIP: Some modern waitlist platforms offer pre-emptive notifications. This means that they notify guests when a table is ready *and* keep them informed throughout the waiting process. For example, as soon as a party of guests settles the bill, a notification is generated for the next party: "*We're clearing your table now. Your estimated remaining wait time is 3 minutes.*" Look for this feature when selecting a waitlist platform or integrating waitlist functionality into your current point-of-sale system.

Remember that the waiting period can be a source of anxiety for diners. Timely digital notifications help alleviate this anxiety by providing a clear and tangible connection to the restaurant's status. Patrons no longer need to wonder when their table will be ready; they receive real-time updates. This allows for efficient communication while offering convenience for both guests and staff.

Personalization is another advantage of digital notifications. You can tailor messages to include the guest's name, expected wait time, and even a warm welcome. These personalized touches further enhance the guest experience and make them feel valued.

PRO TIP: Many aspects of consumer privacy and digital communications are regulated by U.S. and E.U. laws. It is important to familiarize yourself with the rules and limitations of these types of laws. If in doubt, be sure to consult with a lawyer.

Digital notifications have become a valuable tool for modern restaurants to manage their waitlists effectively. By embracing this technology, you can elevate your communication with diners – keeping them informed, engaged, and satisfied throughout their wait. When guests experience this level of service, they are more likely to leave with a positive impression and a desire to return.

Provide Waitlist Management Training

Not surprisingly, your staff's skills, knowledge, and empowerment play a pivotal role in enhancing the overall dining experience. From the hostess who warmly greets waiting patrons to the servers who provide updates and guidance, each member of your team plays a crucial part in ensuring a seamless and pleasant waiting experience for your guests.

Giving your employees the confidence and autonomy to handle situations that may arise during the waitlist process is important. When your staff feels empowered and equipped with the right skills, they become ambassadors of exceptional service. This is because your staff can exert tremendous influence on the perception of your restaurant's brand and work culture.

To begin, start with comprehensive initial training for all staff members involved in waitlist management, from the host or hostess to servers who may interact with waiting guests. Cover essential topics such as greeting procedures, waitlist organization, communication techniques, and conflict resolution.

Consider using simulated scenarios during training to prepare your staff for real-world situations. Simulations can help employees practice handling challenging guests or unexpected delays, boosting their confidence and composure.

PRO TIP: Seasoned staff members can offer guidance from real-world experiences and situations to help provide the foundation for training. Solicit their feedback and input when creating training for new hires and less-tenured staff.

Leverage technology for training purposes. Interactive e-learning modules or training apps can make learning more engaging and accessible for your staff.

Training empowers your staff with knowledge, and knowledge, in turn, breeds confidence. When your staff feels confident in their ability to manage waitlists and interact with waiting guests, it leads to a smoother, more positive experience for everyone involved.

Staff Empowerment and Autonomy

In the context of waitlist management, staff empowerment is a philosophy that elevates staff from mere task performers to problem solvers and powerful brand ambassadors. Empowered staff are not afraid to take initiative, make decisions, and go the extra mile to ensure guest satisfaction.

Empowerment begins with a culture that encourages and values the contributions of your staff. It's about fostering an environment where employees feel trusted, supported, and motivated to take responsibility for the guest experience.

Empowered staff are granted a degree of autonomy for decision-making within established guidelines. For instance, a host or hostess may have the discretion to offer complimentary drinks to waiting guests, or a server may be empowered to resolve minor issues without needing to consult a manager.

When your staff is empowered to address conflicts or guest concerns promptly and effectively, it can diffuse tension and turn a potentially negative experience into a positive one.

Open lines of communication are essential for empowerment. Encourage your staff to provide feedback and suggestions for improvement and actively listen to their insights. When employees feel trusted, confident, and capable of making decisions that enhance the guest experience, it creates a ripple effect of satisfaction and loyalty among your patrons.

Gather and Analyze Data

Let's pivot to another critical aspect of waitlist management – data-driven decision-making. Data collection and analysis can lead to a well-optimized waitlist management process, ensuring that your restaurant consistently delivers exceptional service.

Data comes in many forms, and each piece holds a clue to understanding your guests better. It's not just about numbers; it's about the stories they tell. Every guest interaction, reservation, and wait time can be a piece of this intricate puzzle.

Start by meticulously analyzing reservation data. Note the date and time of each reservation, the number of guests, and any special requests or preferences. This data provides insights into peak hours, popular reservation times, and guest preferences.

PRO TIP: Go one step deeper and cross-reference the reservation data against any specials you're running, local events, or things like holidays or sporting events. Is there a specific reason why reservations are higher than usual? If so, use this to benchmark future reservations so that you're prepared for spikes in guest count. This type of analysis can also guide your marketing strategy.

For walk-in guests, maintain a digital waitlist log. Record the arrival time, the estimated wait time, and any notes about guest preferences or special occasions. This helps you optimize table allocation and accurately predict wait times based on past data.

Finally, be mindful of data privacy regulations. Ensure that you have the necessary permissions to collect and store guest data and implement robust security measures to protect sensitive information.

The collection of data is the foundation upon which data-driven decision-making rests. When you gather and organize data, you equip yourself with the tools needed to analyze guest behavior, optimize waitlist management, and deliver a positive dining experience that leaves a lasting impression.

Focus on Providing a Guest-Centric Experience

Okay. Let's put it all together now and combine the aspects we've discussed to see how to provide a guest-centric experience. We'll start with a deeper dive into managing guest expectations. Then, we'll explore ways to deliver an outstanding experience by looking at situations from the perspective of the customer.

More About Managing Expectations

Managing expectations involves building an atmosphere of transparency and trust. Guests should know what to expect during their visit. Inform them about estimated wait times, table availability, and any special circumstances that may affect their experience. Honesty is your greatest ally, and full transparency is where your restaurant shines.

PRO TIP: Make sure your dine-in customers don't feel devalued by the volume of delivery platform orders, especially during peak dining times. Put yourself in the shoes of the customer – they've taken the time to physically arrive at your restaurant, and are generally prepared to spend more per check than a delivery order (even though the volume of delivery orders may be higher). Be sensitive to their feelings and make them feel valued if they have to wait longer than usual for a table.

Continuously assess your communication strategies, gather feedback from guests, and refine your approach to ensure that expectations are consistently met or exceeded. Striving to exceed expectations is important to ensuring a positive guest experience in your restaurant. Setting the stage with transparency and honesty creates an environment where every guest feels valued and understood.

Offer Alternative Options if Necessary

Sometimes, offering diners alternative options is the only solution to keep them pacified. Being flexible and adaptable in this area is a hallmark of guest-centric thinking.

Begin by highlighting the bar or lounge area as an alternative to being seated at a table. Guests can enjoy drinks and appetizers while waiting, creating a positive experience even during the wait. It's also an excellent opportunity to upsell beverages and appetizers.

Alternatively, suggest a different dining time. If the estimated wait time doesn't suit a guest's schedule, propose alternative time slots when the restaurant is likely to be less crowded. This often helps guests feel in control of their dining experience.

If necessary, promote takeout or delivery options. If the restaurant is exceptionally busy, some guests may prefer to enjoy your cuisine in the comfort of their homes.

PRO TIP: If you opt to suggest takeout or delivery, be sure to offer this option for guests who are calling in to secure a table (not guests already at the restaurant). This will prevent a larger backlog while showing your commitment to the satisfaction of guests who have already arrived.

Consider offering special seating arrangements. If a guest is celebrating a special occasion, offer a more intimate or unique seating option, even if it means a slightly longer wait. This can turn a wait into a memorable part of their dining experience.

If a guest desires a specific table or location within the restaurant, let them join a waiting list. This keeps their anticipation high and shows your commitment to their satisfaction.

Consider offering perks for waiting guests, such as complimentary drinks, appetizers, or discounts for those waiting beyond a certain time. This not only manages expectations but also fosters loyalty.

By offering alternative options, you empower guests to adapt and enjoy their dining experience, even when faced with unexpected twists and challenges. Your commitment to guest satisfaction comes through during these trying situations and will endear customers to your restaurant and your brand.

Why Delivering an Outstanding Experience is Critical

The dining landscape has undergone a profound transformation. Delivery platforms and meal prep services, with their promises of convenience and speed, have changed the way people think about meals. In this new landscape, restaurants aren't the only game in town – so they must rise above the allure of staying home and eating in and, instead, offer an experience that's worth venturing out for.

Never underestimate the power of today's guests, who are discerning and vocal about their experiences. A single positive encounter can lead to glowing reviews, repeat visits, and enthusiastic recommendations. Conversely, a negative experience can ripple through social media and review platforms, deterring potential patrons.

PRO TIP: As I write this book in the winter of 2023, many experts are pointing to a recession on the horizon. During recessions, economic growth slows. People spend less – including dining out. It is critical to go the extra mile with diners during periods of economic slowdown.

Understand the Customer's Point of View

Sometimes, it's helpful to take a step back and put yourself in the shoes of the customer. From their viewpoint, dining choices are everywhere. The rise of instant delivery services offers an enticing shortcut to a satisfying meal without the need to leave home. This means no waiting, no dressing up, no having to deal with strangers, and no need to brave unpredictable weather or traffic. It's dining on their terms.

However, despite the allure of convenience, customers still yearn for the quintessential dining experience that only a restaurant can provide. The ambiance, the aroma, the personal touch—it's an experience that transcends mere sustenance.

The question is, will they choose *your* restaurant?

Diners really seek an emotional connection with both their food and the restaurant that serves it. Dining out is an emotional journey with the potential to foster loyalty and repeat business.

Understanding the customer's perspective is the key to rising above the apparent allure of convenience. It's an opportunity to curate dining experiences that leave a lasting impression, transforming a routine meal into an unforgettable event.

Provide Exceptional Service

As quiet as it's kept, people don't like being at home all the time. A global pandemic and subsequent lockdown have proven this. There are times when they want to be out and about. Therefore, providing exceptional service can be one of your most potent tools to foster loyalty. It's the smiles that greet guests, the attentiveness that anticipates their needs, and the efficiency that ensures a seamless experience.

Exceptional service is really about creating a personal connection with each guest. Tailoring the experience to their preferences and anticipating their desires elevates service to an art form.

Consistently exceeding guest expectations is another aspect. It's about going the extra mile, surprising guests with unexpected delights, and turning ordinary moments into extraordinary memories. These are some of the linchpins that luxury restaurants and hotels live by.

Providing outstanding service is the cornerstone of guest loyalty. A memorable experience is not easily forgotten, and satisfied guests become your most ardent advocates, sharing their tales of exceptional service with friends and family.

In the dining landscape, top-notch service takes center stage. It's the element that transforms a routine visit to your restaurant into a place where unforgettable memories are created. Remember, exceptional service isn't just an act; it's a commitment to excellence that defines your restaurant's identity and ensures its long-term success.

Key Takeaways

While impeccable cuisine and warm ambiance are essential components of a restaurant's allure, the efficient management of your waitlist is an element that cannot be ignored, yet often goes undetected by small restaurant owners.

Ignoring this problem leads many well-intentioned restaurateurs to encounter frustrated customers, missed opportunities, and declining revenue. The restaurant landscape is evolving rapidly, driven by the ever-accelerating pace of modern life and the influence of social media. Today, people are accustomed to one-day delivery times and instant content gratification, which has inevitably influenced their expectations when dining out.

The inability to manage your restaurant's waitlist effectively can prove costly in terms of customer satisfaction in the era of digital interconnectedness, where one negative experience can be broadcast far and wide, potentially tarnishing your restaurant's reputation.

However, the good news is that when done right, waitlist management can become a powerful tool for enhancing your guests' experience and driving repeat business. We discussed best practices, communication strategies, and the role of modern technology in making this happen.

As we conclude this chapter, keep these points in mind:

- The era of instant gratification has conditioned consumers to expect rapid results, and this expectation extends to the dining experience.

- Communication is pivotal in keeping guests happy while waiting for a table. How you manage and engage with them during this crucial period can significantly impact their overall dining experience.

- Ensure your waiting area is clean, comfortable, and aesthetically pleasing to waiting customers.

- Train and empower your staff to be sensitive to the needs of waiting diners. Provide accurate estimated wait times and hold to them.

- Data from past dining experiences is a treasure trove of information about guest behavior, preferences, and the inner workings of your establishment. By analyzing and learning from it, you'll anticipate guest needs and allocate resources effectively.

Let's move on to Mistake #5: Poor Menu Presentation.

Chapter 8
Mistake #5: Poor Menu Presentation

"If anything is good for pounding humility into you permanently, it's the restaurant business."

Anthony Bourdain

We've come to our final item – *Mistake #5: Poor Menu Presentation*.

Now, you might be asking, *"Why did we save this one for last?"*

Well, because in many respects, it's the most important aspect to get right. Many small restaurant owners start listing dishes without much planning or forethought. They simply don't realize that their menu is the most important document in their entire business model.

Your menu has the potential to shape the destiny of your restaurant in ways you may never have imagined. Therefore, failing to give it the proper attention is a mistake that can have serious repercussions.

Your restaurant's menu is the first tangible experience your guests have with your establishment. It sets the stage for what promises to be a memorable dining experience, or, regrettably, a disappointing one. *Mistake #5, the problem of Poor Menu Presentation*, arises when this critical element is neglected, underestimated, or dismissed.

What is Poor Menu Presentation?

Alright, let's cut to the chase here. What exactly is poor menu presentation? It is the problem of presenting your restaurant's menu in a way that fails to captivate, inform, and guide your guests effectively.

The issue is not just the aesthetics (although that plays a significant role). Instead, it encompasses the entire experience your menu offers, from its visual appeal to its ability to simplify choices and enhance the guest experience.

Think of your menu as a storyteller, setting the stage for the dining experience your guests are about to embark upon. A well-presented menu should do more than list dishes and prices. It should allow your diners to taste with their mind . . . it should be a prelude to the multitude of flavors your kitchen is ready to produce.

But what happens when *Mistake #5* creeps in?

The menu loses its narrative power and becomes a dry, boring catalog. It fails to engage diners or guide them toward the culinary options your restaurant offers. The consequences of this can be subtle yet profound.

Unclear menus often leave guests bewildered and frustrated, making the dining experience feel more like a riddle to be solved than a pleasure to be savored. They might struggle to decipher menu choices, leading to indecision and potentially an underwhelming meal. It's an unfortunate scenario where your menu, instead of being an ally, becomes an obstacle to guest satisfaction.

Now, you might wonder, "*Does the design of a menu truly matter that much?*"

The answer is a resounding *"Yes"*.

Your Menu is Integral to the Dining Experience

A poorly presented menu may cast doubt on the professionalism and quality of your restaurant. It can undermine the carefully crafted image you've built for your business, eroding brand perception and potentially deterring repeat business.

Conversely, A well-crafted menu can set the tone, arouse anticipation, and leave a lasting impression on your guests. Upon opening the menu, your goal is to make guests feel thrilled and engrossed by the culinary possibilities.

People eat with their minds long before their taste buds are engaged. Therefore, your menu is the gateway to their culinary adventure, the bridge between anticipation and fulfillment.

Here are some additional factors that make menus so integral to the dining experience.

- **Building Anticipation and Excitement:** A well-designed menu ignites excitement and curiosity in your guests. It's the first encounter with your cuisine, and it should leave them eager to explore what your kitchen has to offer.

- **Guest Engagement:** Effective menu presentation engages your guests in the dining experience from the moment they sit down. It draws them into your restaurant's story and helps them connect with your culinary identity.

- **Decision-Making:** The menu should be a guiding light for your guests, helping them make choices that align with their preferences and desires. A clear and well-structured menu can streamline decision-making and ensure that guests have a satisfying experience.

- **Setting Expectations:** Your menu sets expectations for the meal ahead. It conveys the level of sophistication, the style of cuisine, and the overall vibe of your restaurant.

- **Branding:** Beyond the food itself, your menu is a branding tool. It communicates your restaurant's personality, values, and unique selling points.

As we continue our journey, you'll see how an effective menu is a delicate balance of design, psychology, and storytelling. In the sections ahead, we'll go deeper into the intricacies of menu design, uncovering the strategies and techniques that transform your menu into an engaging and indispensable part of your restaurant's success.

What Happens When Diners View Subpar Menus?

In the next section, we'll dive into the consequences of poor menu presentation, but I wanted to touch on a few key aspects first. It's important to consider what goes through the minds of your diners when they look at your menu. The impact of a poorly presented menu has a ripple effect, leaving a lasting imprint on your restaurant's trajectory.

Here are a few ways this can adversely affect your restaurant:

- **Guest Dissatisfaction and Frustration:** A menu that feels more like a cryptic puzzle than a culinary guide, poorly designed, cluttered, and confusing, can lead to guest dissatisfaction and frustration. It hinders the very essence of the dining experience by causing indecision and potentially resulting in unsatisfying choices.

- **Guest Loyalty and Repeat Business:** Dissatisfied guests are less likely to return, and they may share their negative experiences with others. This not only impacts immediate revenue but also hinders the growth of a loyal customer base. A poorly presented menu can drive potential repeat business away.

- **Undermined Professionalism:** A poorly presented menu can inadvertently convey an impression of unprofessionalism and lack of attention to detail. Guests may question the quality and professionalism of the entire establishment, and this doubt can cast a shadow over the entire dining experience.

- **Negative Brand Perception:** Your menu is an extension of your restaurant's brand. When it falls short in terms of presentation, it tarnishes the carefully cultivated image you've worked so hard to build. A menu that doesn't reflect the values and standards of your restaurant can leave a negative imprint on your brand perception.

PRO TIP: The guest experience is far more emotional than tangible. Many times, guests leave a bad review, not because of the food, but because of things like buyer friction and menu confusion. Most often, this negative perception occurs at a subconscious level.

Remember that investing in your menu is a strategic decision that directly influences the success and longevity of your restaurant. It's a powerful tool that, when wielded correctly, can elevate your guest experience, enhance your brand, and ensure that every diner leaves with a positive impression.

Okay, let's move on to a deeper dive into the consequences of poor menu presentation.

Consequences of Poor Menu Presentation

Each aspect of your menu design, from its layout to its visual elements, plays an important role in shaping the guest experience. Let's start to unravel the impact of *Mistake #5* in greater detail, dissecting it into three major categories:

1. **The Impact of Unclear Menus:** We'll explore how unclear menus can lead to guest dissatisfaction and frustration, turning the dining experience into a perplexing puzzle.

2. **Impact on Server Efficiency:** You'll learn how menu presentation can influence a server's ability to guide guests efficiently and take orders without a hitch. We'll examine the potential for increased wait times and how these can erode your restaurant's table turnover.

3. **Influence on Brand Perception:** We'll explore how a poorly presented menu can cast a shadow on your restaurant's image, conveying a negative impression that extends far beyond the dining room. We'll also discuss the role of menus in shaping your restaurant's brand identity and reputation.

Through these 3 sections, you'll gain a deep understanding of how every detail in your menu design can either work in your favor or against you. These consequences can quickly ripple through your operations, affecting guest satisfaction, server performance, and the very essence of your brand.

The Impact of Unclear Menus

Poorly designed menus leave diners scratching their heads rather than salivating over choices. This can have a deep impact on their overall experience.

Here's why clarity in menu presentation matters:

- **Guest Bewilderment:** When a menu's dish descriptions are vague, and the organization is chaotic, it feels like an intellectual challenge rather than a pleasurable dining experience. Unclear menus can leave guests confused and frustrated.

- **Indecision and Suboptimal Choices:** When faced with an unclear menu, guests may struggle to make decisions. They may even choose dishes at random out of sheer confusion. This can lead to suboptimal choices, where diners don't order what they truly desire, resulting in an underwhelming dining experience. The worst part is that they may provide a bad review based on *their* choice.

- **Dining Delays and Reduced Table Turnover:** Inefficiencies in ordering due to unclear menus can lead to longer wait times for both guests and servers. This not only tests the patience of diners but also reduces the table turnover rate, potentially impacting your restaurant's revenue.

- **Guest Retention Challenges:** Diners commonly associate confusing menus with an unsatisfactory experience. Unsatisfied guests are less likely to return to your restaurant and often share their negative experiences with others. This can hinder the development of a loyal customer base and impede your restaurant's growth.

Dining out should be a joyful and memorable experience. Your guests come to your restaurant to discover new flavors, savor delicious dishes, and share memorable moments. A vague or confusing menu casts a shadow over the entire experience.

The Impact on Server Efficiency

Now, for a moment, put yourself in the shoes of your server.

As you quickly shuffle between tables, you're ready to assist and guide your guests in making their dining choices. You're the bridge between the kitchen and the dining room, ensuring that each guest's experience is seamless and enjoyable. But guests often linger, asking you to "*come back later... we'll need a few more minutes to decide.*"

Picture this scenario: A guest opens the menu, and their brow furrows as they attempt to decipher the dishes. The font is minuscule, the descriptions vague, and the layout chaotic. They turn to the server, seeking clarity and guidance.

Your server now faces a daunting task. They must interpret the menu for the guest (or several guests per table), explaining what each dish entails, its ingredients, and potential substitutions. Minutes tick by as they decide. This not only prolongs the interaction but also increases the chances of miscommunication.

For your restaurant to run smoothly, time is of the essence. Efficient service is paramount, but a cumbersome or confusing menu can silently undermine efficiency. When guests struggle with the menu, it takes longer for them to make decisions. They may request additional time, flip through pages, or ask numerous questions out of fear of making a bad decision.

This can lead to longer table turnover times, potentially reducing the number of guests your restaurant can accommodate in a given evening. It also places additional stress on your servers, as they strive to manage multiple tables while assisting guests who are grappling with an unclear menu.

Conversely, a well-structured menu can also be a powerful tool for upselling—encouraging guests to explore additional menu items to enhance their dining experience. But a menu that lacks visual appeal or fails to highlight special features or high-profit menu items can hinder your ability to suggest add-ons or upgrades.

When the menu itself doesn't entice guests to explore beyond their initial choices, you may miss opportunities to increase the average check size.

Your server's role is not just to take orders, but also to enhance your guests' dining experience by providing guidance and recommendations. An unclear menu can make this a challenge. It can transform their role from a knowledgeable guide to a translator of menu jargon, prolonging each guest interaction.

Increased Wait Times & Decreased Table Turnover

During service, time is both your ally and your adversary. Every minute counts and the balance between attentive service and prompt table turnover is a delicate one. Yet, the way a menu is presented can tip this balance, potentially leading to increased wait times and decreased table turnover rates.

As guests wrestle with a confusing menu, they naturally take longer to make decisions, and servers must patiently await their choices. This extended decision-making process not only affects the table you're serving but also has a ripple effect throughout your restaurant. Other diners who have already placed their orders may begin to grow impatient, leading to potential complaints or diminished guest satisfaction.

Increased wait times for order placement can set off a chain reaction that negatively impacts your restaurant's performance. Longer stays at tables mean reduced table turnover, which, in turn, can affect your restaurant's capacity to accommodate new guests.

This domino effect can lead to:

- **Reduced Revenue:** Longer table turnover times mean fewer opportunities to serve new guests, potentially translating into a decrease in daily revenue.

- **Increased Labor Costs:** Servers may find themselves spending more time at each table, leading to higher labor costs without a corresponding increase in revenue.

- **Resource Allocation Challenges:** Kitchen and service staff must adapt to the extended table occupancy, which can strain resources and impact overall efficiency.

Efficient table turnover is a key metric in the restaurant industry, as it directly influences both revenue and guest satisfaction. Therefore, addressing menu-related issues that contribute to increased wait times is not just a matter of convenience but a strategic imperative.

Influence on Brand Perception

Perception creates reality. Your brand is not just your logo or your sign over the door; it's the collective impression guests form during their visit to your establishment. Every element, from the decor to the service, contributes to this perception, and the menu is no exception.

As a restaurant owner, understanding this connection is crucial. Your brand is your promise to your guests, and the menu is one of the most tangible expressions of that promise. Whether you aim to convey sophistication, comfort, or innovation, your menu plays a pivotal role in shaping these impressions.

Think of your menu as the cover of a book—often the first thing your guests encounter, and their initial judgment of what lies within. When your menu has design flaws, cluttered layouts, or outdated aesthetics, it sends a message to your guests.

Here's how a poorly presented menu creates a negative brand perception:

- **Perceived Neglect:** An outdated or worn menu can suggest neglect, causing guests to wonder if the same lack of care extends to the kitchen and the overall dining experience.

- **Confusion Breeds Skepticism:** A menu riddled with inconsistencies, "cheffy" jargon, typos, or unclear descriptions can lead guests to question the professionalism and attention to detail within the restaurant.

- **Undermining Quality:** A haphazard menu design can subtly undermine the perception of food quality, leaving guests skeptical about the culinary experience.

Imagine your guests flipping through a menu and encountering a sea of text, inconsistent fonts, or poor-quality images. Their first impression might be one of disarray and indifference on the part of the restaurant. This can color their entire dining experience.

Your menu extends beyond the physical realm. Many guests explore your offerings online before making a reservation or stepping through your restaurant's doors. A poorly designed website or digital menu can have the same negative impact, turning potential guests away before they even set foot inside.

Influence on Brand Identity and Reputation

Closely linked with brand perception (what others think of your brand) is brand identity (how your brand uniquely identifies your restaurant). Think of your menu as a brand ambassador that communicates your restaurant's essence, values, and unique offerings. Every choice you make in menu design—colors, fonts, images, and descriptions—contributes to this message.

Here are some ways menus influence brand identity and reputation:

- **Visual Identity:** The design and aesthetics of your menu should echo your restaurant's visual identity, reinforcing the recognition of your brand. Whether it's a sleek, modern design or a rustic, cozy feel, your menu design should align with your restaurant's ambiance.

- **Culinary Narrative:** The menu is a platform for storytelling, where each dish description weaves a narrative about your cuisine and the passion that goes into creating it. It's a chance to convey your commitment to quality, innovation, or tradition.

- **Consistency:** A cohesive menu design across all touchpoints—physical menus, websites, and social media—builds trust and reinforces your brand voice. Inconsistencies can leave guests wondering if they've entered the right restaurant.

The menu also sets the stage for guest expectations and experiences. It's not just about what you serve but how you present it. For example, a menu with elegant descriptions and sophisticated layouts sets the expectation of a fine dining experience (with prices to match). However, if the menu misrepresents what you deliver, it can lead to disappointment and tarnish your restaurant's reputation. Consistency between the promise made by your menu and the reality on the plate is essential.

Menu Presentation Best Practices

We've explored how menu presentation can influence table turnover, guest satisfaction, and brand perception. Now, it's time to roll up our sleeves and explore some practical aspects of designing menus that not only look stunning but also enhance the dining experience.

In this section, we'll look at the art and science behind menu design, providing you with practical tips to create menus that leave an indelible mark on your guests.

We'll touch on the following topics:

- **Guidelines for Creating Menus:** A comprehensive guide on layout, typography, and imagery, ensuring that your menu is both visually appealing and easy to navigate.

- **Simplifying Choices:** Strategies to streamline your menu offerings, avoiding overwhelming guests with too many options while maximizing their enjoyment.

- **Enhancing the Guest Experience:** Techniques to elevate your menu into a storytelling platform, turning each dish into a chapter of your restaurant's unique narrative.

- **Contributing to Efficient Table Turnover:** Insights into how a well-structured menu can expedite the ordering process, reduce service time, and boost revenue.

Let's begin.

Design A Visually Appealing & Easy-to-Read Menu

Think of the menu as your restaurant's manifesto. It's a reflection of your restaurant's identity and a bridge connecting your kitchen with the eager palates of your guests.

To begin, there are 3 core elements of a well-crafted menu.

- **Layout and Structure:** The fundamental architecture of your menu, ensures it's easy to navigate and visually engaging.

- **Typography and Fonts:** The choice of fonts that convey your restaurant's personality and aid readability.

- **Imagery:** The power of high-quality images to entice and inspire your guests.

The guidelines we'll cover are tried-and-true strategies employed by successful restaurateurs to create menus that not only look stunning but also contribute to efficient service and higher revenue.

Let's start with a 5-step process for creating a menu that not only whets the appetite but also ensures a smooth and enjoyable ordering experience:

Step 1: Start with a Well-Structured Layout

Think of your menu as a roadmap for your guests. A well-structured layout guides their eyes, allowing them to navigate your dishes with minimal effort.

Here are some tips.

- **Sections and Categories:** Organize your menu into logical sections or categories. Group similar dishes together, whether by course, cuisine type, or dietary preference. This helps guests quickly find what they're looking for.

PRO TIP: The layout of your sections and categories is one of the most important things to get right. Make sure that your section layout is consistent between courses, cuisine types, dietary preferences, and allergen information.

- **Hierarchy:** Use a hierarchy of fonts, sizes, and colors to emphasize key elements, such as dish names, descriptions, and prices. Make sure the most important information is easily distinguishable.

- **White Space:** Don't underestimate the power of white space. It creates breathing room, prevents visual clutter, and enhances readability. Ensure there's enough space between each menu item and between sections.

Step 2: Choose Readable Fonts that Complement your Theme

The choice of fonts can significantly impact how easily your menu can be read.

Consider these tips.

- **Legibility:** Prioritize legibility over artistic flair. Opt for fonts that are clear and easy to read, even in low-light conditions. If your restaurant features a dimly lit, intimate atmosphere for dinner, make sure that the menu is legible in candlelight, or other dimly-lit spaces.

PRO TIP: More people than you realize have vision-related disabilities, or suffer from low vision. This can be even more common for older diners, or those who work in computer-related fields. Although the revenue potential can be higher among these groups, visual clarity is more important. Customers should not feel like they're taking an eyeglasses test when they read the menu. Try taking the menu to each table and look at it from 3 feet away in a low-light condition (not during the day when more light is available).

- **Consistency:** Stick to a limited number of fonts, ideally two—one for headings and one for body text. Consistency in fonts maintains a clean and cohesive appearance. Also consider the fonts used across all your branding materials, from menus to websites, to ensure a cohesive and memorable brand identity.

- **Brand Identity:** Fonts also contribute to your brand's identity. They can convey whether your restaurant is casual, upscale, traditional, or modern. Think about the message you want to convey. Fonts can also subtly tell a story about the food you serve. For example, using an old-western font for a Texas BBQ restaurant fits both the cuisine and brand identity.

PRO TIP: When selecting a font, think carefully about branding. Think about the message you want to convey. Serif fonts may evoke tradition and elegance, while sans-serif fonts can signify modernity and simplicity.

Step 3: Highlight Key Information

When planning your menu, make sure that essential information stands out to the reader and can be found quickly.

For example:

- **Dish Names:** Use a larger or bolder font for dish names to draw attention. This helps guests quickly identify dishes.

- **Prices:** Prices should be easy to find and read. Typically, they are aligned to the right for quick scanning.

- **Descriptions:** Use concise, evocative descriptions that capture the essence of each dish. Consider placing descriptions in a slightly smaller font under dish names.

PRO TIP: When describing dishes, don't use a lot of "cheffy" jargon. This can quickly confuse guests. This is prevalent in a lot of high-end restaurants. People don't like to feel stupid when they read a restaurant menu.

Step 4: Quality Imagery Matters

Visual appeal plays a pivotal role in menu design, and high-quality images are the gateway to your guests' hearts and palates. If you include images of your dishes, ensure they are high-quality.

Here's why it matters and some practical tips for captivating imagery:

- **Appetite Stimulation:** Research suggests that visual imagery can stimulate the appetite and influence diners' choices. A beautifully captured image of a dish can be the nudge that leads to an order.

- **Storytelling:** Images tell stories about your cuisine. They can convey the essence of your dishes, whether it's the sizzle of a steak, the creamy texture of a dessert, or the freshness of a salad.

- **Trust Building:** High-quality images communicate professionalism and attention to detail. They reassure your guests that the dishes they see are what they'll receive.

- **Professional Photography:** If possible, invest in professional food photography to showcase your dishes in the best light.

PRO TIP: Think of your images as digital assets. Once purchased, they can be repurposed for use on your website, social media, ad campaigns, etc. Investing the time and money to get them right will save money in the long run.

- **Consistent Style:** Maintain a consistent style for your images to create visual harmony. Consistency reinforces your brand identity and guides guests' expectations.

Step 5: Keep It Clean and Uncluttered

Less is often more when it comes to menu design.

- **Limited Choices:** Avoid overwhelming guests with an excessively long menu. Focus on quality over quantity.

- **Minimalist Design:** Embrace minimalist design principles to keep your menu clean and uncluttered.

Remember, your menu should be a guide, not an obstacle. These practical tips help ensure that it enhances the dining experience, making it seamless and pleasurable for your guests.

Before moving on to Menu Simplicity, let's lay the foundation by talking about Psychology in dining.

The Psychology of Choice: A Key Ingredient in Menu Design

The choices we make as consumers are not merely based on taste preferences but are deeply influenced by psychological factors that underpin the process of decision-making. Understanding the psychology of choice is a critical ingredient in crafting menus that resonate with diners.

In this supplementary section, we'll take a quick detour and look at how the human mind navigates the culinary landscape, and we'll provide insights into how this knowledge can be used to create menus that captivate your diners.

Understanding "The Paradox of Choice"

Renowned psychologist Barry Schwartz introduced the concept of the *"paradox of choice,"* which suggests that while we tend to believe that more options lead to greater satisfaction, an abundance of choices actually has the opposite effect — it can often overwhelm and paralyze decision-making.

In a restaurant setting, this is particularly relevant. When menus are excessively long and intricate, guests may feel burdened with choices, leading to frustration or even decision avoidance.

Okay. Let's move on to price perception — another element of psychology at play.

"Anchoring" and Price Perception

The human mind has a natural tendency to rely on the first piece of information encountered when making decisions—a cognitive bias known as *"anchoring."*

In the context of menus, the way prices are presented can significantly influence guests' perception of value. For instance, strategically placing a high-priced item at the top of a menu can make other items seem more affordable in comparison.

Emotional Resonance and Storytelling

The emotional connection guests have with a dish can play a pivotal role in their decision-making process. This is where the art of storytelling comes into play.

Descriptions that evoke sensory experiences, cultural narratives, or personal anecdotes can transform a dish from a mere list of ingredients into a captivating, emotionally charged story.

Menu Layout and Decision Flow

The layout of a menu can guide guests through the decision-making process. The *"Golden Triangle"* principle suggests that when dining, a guest's eyes are naturally drawn to the center, then the top right of a menu.

As they continue to scan, their eyes drift to the left of the menu. Items strategically placed within this zone tend to receive more attention.

By understanding this, you can highlight specific dishes you want to promote. For example, consider placing specials, high-profit items, or items that are quick to prepare in these *"zones."*

The Golden Triangle Concept in menu design

The Power of Social Influence and Recommendations

Social factors significantly impact dining choices. Guests are often easily influenced by the choices of their peers, both in terms of dish selection and ordering behavior.

Highlighting *"chef's recommendations"* or *"most popular"* items can also leverage social influence to guide choices.

Incorporating an understanding of psychological principles into menu design can be a game-changer for your restaurant. By aligning menu offerings with the way the human mind processes choices, you can create a dining experience that satisfies appetites while also leaving guests with a sense of fulfillment and delight.

Okay. Now that we've covered human psychology let's move on to designing a menu from the ground up with simplicity in mind.

Design Menus with Simplicity in Mind

The art of simplifying your menu is similar to working with high-quality proteins – trimming the excess while preserving the good stuff. Let's explore some strategies and techniques to transform complex menus into concise, guest-friendly experiences.

Imagine hungry guests scrolling through page after page of mouthwatering dishes, each more tempting than the last. But as they flip through the seemingly endless options, a feeling of overwhelm creeps in.

Sound familiar?

This is the paradox of choice in action—when more options lead to less satisfaction.

As discussed in the prior section, research suggests that too many choices can paralyze decision-making and leave guests feeling dissatisfied with their selections. In your quest to provide variety, you may inadvertently overwhelm your guests. Streamlining your menu is the antidote to choice overload.

How to Streamline Your Menu

First, understand that specialization is the art of doing a few things exceptionally well. Instead of offering an extensive menu with countless dishes, focus on a curated selection of signature items that capture the essence of your brand. This not only simplifies choices for your guests but also allows your kitchen to focus on executing these dishes to perfection.

Scan your menu for redundancy. Are there multiple dishes with similar ingredients or flavor profiles? Consider consolidating these into a single, standout item that captures the essence of the group. Not only does this declutter your menu, but it also highlights your restaurant's unique strengths.

Also, consider offering a seasonal menu that changes periodically. This not only keeps your menu fresh and exciting but also reduces the number of items your guests need to choose from at any given time.

Identify your restaurant's signature dishes or customer favorites and place them in a prominent position on your menu. These are your menu stars—the dishes that define your culinary identity. Guests often appreciate having a few standout options to consider.

Introduce limited-time specials that align with your restaurant's theme or current culinary trends. These items can add an element of excitement without overwhelming your regular menu.

A streamlined menu is not about limiting choice but enhancing it. By simplifying options, you empower your guests to make decisions more quickly and comfortably. A concise menu also enables your kitchen staff to excel in creating each dish, ensuring consistently outstanding quality.

As you streamline your menu, remember that quality should always prevail over quantity. Each item on your menu should shine, representing the best of your culinary vision. When done right, a well-curated menu simplifies choices, making the dining experience more delightful and memorable.

How to Categorize and Organize Menu Items

Not only is it important to know what to put on the menu, it is equally important to know where to place menu items. In this section, we'll look at categorization and organization—a crucial aspect of streamlining your menu while enhancing the guest's journey.

Think of your menu as a map, and categories as signposts guiding your guests. Effective categorization simplifies the decision-making process by offering a clear structure for exploration.

Here are some practical tips:

- **Logical Grouping:** Group similar dishes together under well-defined categories. For example, if your restaurant offers various pasta dishes, create a "Pasta Delights" category. This approach makes it easy for guests to navigate and compare options.

- **Establish a Hierarchy of Information:** Establish a hierarchy within your categories by strategically placing your standout dishes at the top. These dishes can serve as anchors, capturing the guest's attention and setting the tone for their dining experience.

- **Add Sensory Appeal:** Appeal to your guests' senses by creating categories that evoke emotions and sensations. For instance, using action words like "Sizzling Steaks" or "Decadent Desserts" can trigger anticipation and excitement.

- **Dietary Considerations:** Incorporate categories that cater to specific dietary preferences or requirements. Include headings like "Gluten-Free Delights" or "Vegetarian Extravaganza" to accommodate various dining needs and allergies.

- **Visual Harmony:** The visual presentation of your categories is just as important as their content. Remember the core design elements: Clear Typography, Consistency, White Space, and Imagery.

When done right, categories streamline the decision-making process, guiding guests to memorable dining experiences. Remember, your menu empowers your guests to explore your dishes with confidence and anticipation. Thoughtful categorization is a key component in crafting a menu that captivates and inspires.

Use Your Menu to Enhance the Guest Experience

Every meal is a story waiting to be told—flavors, textures, and sensations leave a lasting impression. Let's explore how menu design can transcend the *"functional"* aspects and become a vehicle for storytelling, surprise, and delight.

We'll look at 4 key areas:

- **The Power of Storytelling:** How using words and descriptions can weave tales that transport your guests to faraway lands or evoke cherished memories.

- **Highlighting Special Features:** The art of showcasing unique dishes, seasonal delights, or chef's specialties that elevate your menu to a curated collection of exceptional experiences.

- **Creating Visual Appeal:** How to use imagery and layout to ignite the senses, tantalizing your guests even before their first bite.

- **Personalized Touches:** The art of customization, and how tailoring your menu to your guests' preferences can create moments of true connection with your brand.

Your menu is an invitation to savor, celebrate, and share moments that linger in memory long after the meal is finished. As a restaurant owner, your passion shines through every dish you serve. But now, let's channel that passion into your menu, using it to captivate and inspire your guests.

The Power of Storytelling

I have to admit. I love a great story.

Don't you?

Think of your menu as a story waiting to be told. Words have the incredible ability to transport your guests to a different time or place, to evoke memories, or to ignite their imagination.

Here's how to harness the power of storytelling in your menu.

- **Evocative Descriptions:** Create descriptions that tantalize the senses. Instead of simply listing ingredients, use vivid language to paint a picture of the dish's aroma, flavor, and texture.

- **Use Cultural Narratives:** Infuse your menu with cultural narratives that celebrate the origins of your dishes. Share the heritage, traditions, and stories behind each dish.

- **Personal Anecdotes:** Consider sharing personal anecdotes or experiences related to specific dishes. Guests love knowing that a particular dish has a special place in your heart, or that it's a cherished family recipe.

Highlight Special Features

Highlighting special features on your menu creates excitement and anticipation, making the dining experience all the more special.

Here are some suggestions:

- **Chef's Specials:** Designate a section for "*Chef's Specials*" or "*Chef's Recommendations.*" These are dishes that your kitchen takes pride in, and they deserve a prominent place on your menu.

- **Seasonal Delights:** Celebrate the changing seasons with a dedicated section for seasonal dishes. This not only showcases your restaurant's commitment to freshness but also entices guests with limited-time offerings.

- **Signature Cocktails:** If your establishment offers alcoholic beverages, don't forget to include standout cocktails that complement your menu. A well-crafted cocktail can be a memorable part of the dining experience.

Creating Visual Appeal

The aesthetics and visual elements play a crucial role in enhancing the overall dining experience.

Consider these design tips:

- **Use High-Quality Imagery:** As mentioned earlier, include high-resolution images of your dishes. These visuals should be so enticing that they almost leap off the page.

- **Consistent Design Themes:** Maintain a consistent design theme throughout your menu. Cohesive layouts convey professionalism and attention to detail.

- **Strategic Placement:** Use layout and design to guide the guest's eye. Place dishes with higher profit margins or signature dishes strategically to draw attention.

- **Simplicity and Clarity:** While visual appeal is important, ensure that the menu remains easy to read and navigate. Clarity and simplicity should never be sacrificed for aesthetics.

Remember, your menu is a canvas for storytelling and a showcase for your restaurant's dishes. By infusing your menu with the art of storytelling and effectively highlighting special features, you elevate your guests' experience.

How Menu Design Contributes to Efficient Table Turnover

Efficient table turnover isn't about rushing guests; it's about optimizing for both your patrons and your business. It's a balancing act that ensures your restaurant remains vibrant, profitable, and in demand.

Getting it right is a delicate balance. It's about ensuring that guests enjoy a memorable dining experience while allowing your restaurant to welcome new patrons. A critical element in achieving this equilibrium lies in your menu design.

Expediting the Order Process

Here's how a clear menu design can expedite the ordering process:

- **Clear Organization:** A menu should be organized logically, with sections and categories that make sense. Guests should effortlessly find what they're looking for, whether it's appetizers, entrees, or beverages.

- **Concise Descriptions:** Menu descriptions should be concise yet informative. They should convey the essence of a dish without overwhelming the guest with unnecessary details. This clarity speeds up the decision-making process.

- **Visual Cues:** Strategic use of fonts, colors, and formatting can draw attention to key dishes or specials, helping guests make choices more quickly.

- **Logical Flow:** The menu should follow a logical flow, guiding guests from starters to mains to desserts. This ensures that guests order efficiently without backtracking.

Reduced Service Times Between Courses

In addition to expediting ordering times, having a clear, concise menu also reduces service times between courses, contributing to a quicker table turnover.

Here's how:

- **Accurate Orders:** A well-organized menu layout helps servers take orders accurately and promptly. It minimizes errors and ensures that dishes are prepared and served efficiently.

- **Expedited Communication:** Effective menu design can facilitate communication between the kitchen and servers, reducing the chances of mistakes and ensuring that dishes are prepared and served promptly.

- **Upselling Opportunities:** As we will discuss in the next section, strategic placement of high-margin items or specials can encourage upselling without prolonging the ordering process. Guests may be more inclined to explore additional options.

A well-structured menu simplifies choices, expedites the ordering process, and reduces service time, all without compromising the quality of the guest experience. Efficiency doesn't mean rushing diners; it means ensuring that they have a smooth and enjoyable dining experience while allowing your restaurant to accommodate a steady flow of guests.

Your Menu is a Sales Tool: Upselling, Decision-Making and Faster Service

Let's switch gears to another important benefit of investing in your menu – more money. Your menu not only contributes to faster table turnover but it can also be used as a tool to encourage upselling. In this section, we'll explore how strategic menu design can encourage upselling and quick decision-making, optimizing both your guest's experience and your restaurant's revenue.

Incorporate Upselling into Your Menu

Let's take a step back and clarify what we mean by "upselling". There are many definitions, but I like this one from Salesforce:

> *"Upselling is a sales strategy that involves encouraging customers to buy a higher-end version of a product than what they originally intended to purchase."* [1]
>
> Salesforce

---

1. https://www.salesforce.com/eu/learning-centre/sales/upselling/

Do you ever think of your restaurant menu as a sales tool?

If not, you should.

In fact, your restaurant menu is the most powerful sales tool you have. When done right, it can be leveraged to generate more money per customer.

Upselling is an art, and your menu can be used to guide your guests toward choices that enhance their dining experience while benefiting your bottom line.

Here are a couple of tips.

- **Spotlighting Specials:** Highlighting daily specials or chef's recommendations with eye-catching visuals or callout boxes can pique curiosity and encourage guests to explore beyond their usual choices. For example, showcase daily specials with vivid images and descriptions. These visual cues not only capture attention but also ignite the desire to try something unique and extraordinary.

- **Offer Pairing Suggestions:** Offering pairing suggestions, such as recommending a wine that complements a dish, can enhance the dining experience and increase sales. For example, accompany the description of each dish with a carefully selected wine suggestion, creating an opportunity for guests to explore new flavors and elevate their meals.

Guide the Decision-Making Process

Many times, customers want to make a decision, but the fear of loss and possible embarrassment from not understanding the choices can lead to indecision.

Here's how your menu can help expedite the decision-making process:

- **Icons & Symbols:** The strategic use of icons or symbols can convey information quickly. For instance, a chili pepper icon indicates a spicy dish, while a clock icon can denote a quick-to-prepare option. This allows guests to make decisions swiftly based on their preferences and time constraints.

- **Menu Callouts:** Drawing attention to dishes that are popular or quick to prepare through callout boxes or strategically placed text can guide guests toward choices that streamline the kitchen's workflow.

- **Logical Order Sequencing:** Strategic placement of dishes on the menu can influence the sequence in which they are ordered, facilitating a smooth workflow in the kitchen. For example, many restaurants put appetizers and soups at the beginning of their menu, followed by mains and desserts. This thoughtful layout encourages guests to order courses sequentially, ensuring that the kitchen can prepare and serve dishes in a logical sequence.

Remember that the goal is not to rush your guests, but to enhance their experience by offering enticing choices that align with their preferences and pace. By incorporating upselling strategies and facilitating quick decision-making, your menu supports a more streamlined and enjoyable dining experience, contributing to efficient table turnover without compromising guest satisfaction.

Key Takeaways

In this chapter, we discussed in-depth the fifth critical mistake: *Poor Menu Presentation*. We explored its definition and its far-reaching consequences. We also discussed invaluable insights into menu presentation best practices, guiding you through the art of creating menus that not only simplify choices but contribute to a memorable dining experience.

Remember, your menu is not just a list of dishes; it's a reflection of your restaurant's identity, a silent storyteller that influences guests' decisions and perceptions. By optimizing your menu presentation, you've taken a significant step toward operational efficiency.

Throughout this chapter, we discussed:

- The importance of clear menu organization and the role it plays in guest satisfaction and server efficiency.

- How to avoid guest dissatisfaction and frustration caused by unclear menus.

- The impact of menu design on your restaurant's brand perception and reputation.

- Practical tips for designing menus that are visually appealing and easy to read.

- The significance of using high-quality images and fonts that match your restaurant's theme.

- Strategies for simplifying choices and organizing items effectively.

- How menu design can enhance the overall dining experience through storytelling and highlighting special features.

- The crucial role of a well-structured menu in expediting the ordering process and reducing service time.

You've also explored the psychology of choice as it pertains to dining and menu item selection, deepening your understanding of how guests make decisions when perusing your menu.

Lastly, you discovered how to leverage menu design to encourage upselling and quick decision-making, ensuring that your guests enjoy a seamless dining experience without unnecessary delays.

As you continue to refine your menu design skills, keep in mind that it's an ongoing process. Stay attuned to your guests' feedback, monitor the effectiveness of your menu changes, and adapt to evolving trends.

Now that we've covered the 5 table turnover mistakes, it's time to look at some additional operational strategies that can help your restaurant. We'll cover these in the next section.

SECTION 3

Staff Training, Technology, Social Media & Reputation Management

In this section, I'll share some additional insights to other operational aspects that can help your small business thrive in the post-COVID economy. Namely, we'll cover social media, the importance of technology solutions and their implementation, training, and reputation management.

These aspects will round out our discussion and supplement the strategies given in the prior chapters.

CHAPTER 9
Staff Training and Customer Service

"Every contact we have with a customer influences whether or not they'll come back. We have to be great every time or we'll lose them."

Kevin Stirtz

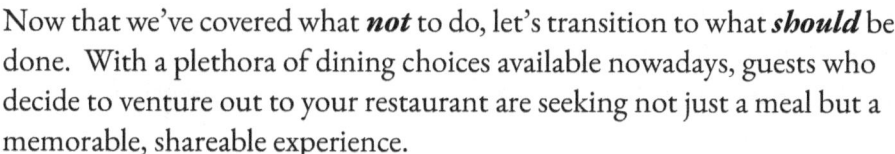

Now that we've covered what **not** to do, let's transition to what **should** be done. With a plethora of dining choices available nowadays, guests who decide to venture out to your restaurant are seeking not just a meal but a memorable, shareable experience.

As such, the role of your staff is pivotal. They are your restaurant's face, voice, and heartbeat. Their interactions with guests can make or break a dining experience and, in turn, influence your restaurant's table turnover rates and profitability.

Here, we look at the art and science of staff training and customer service excellence, revealing the secrets that enhance the quality of service your restaurant provides and significantly impact your bottom line.

Let's start with why staff training is so critical to long-term success.

The Importance of Staff Training

In the hustle and bustle of running a restaurant, it's easy to overlook the significance of staff training. After all, you might think that hiring a team of experienced servers and cooks should be enough to keep your establishment afloat. However, the reality is that staff training is that it's the cornerstone of delivering exceptional customer service.

> "From front-of-house servers to kitchen staff, proper training ensures that every team member understands their responsibilities and can perform their tasks effectively... By investing in training, restaurant owners can build a team that is confident, competent, and capable of delivering exceptional service consistently."[1]

In this section, we'll examine how staff training lays the foundation for giving your restaurant a reputation for exceptional service. Then, we'll transition into how training plays into meeting guest expectations, and finally, we'll look at the ways in which training drives consistency.

---

1. 1huddle: Investing in Your Team: The Benefits of Training Programs for Restaurant Staff. https://1huddle.co/blog/investing-in-your-team-the-benefits-of-training-programs-for-restaurant-staff/

Training Lays the Foundation for Exceptional Service

Imagine a guest walks through your restaurant's doors and is greeted by a server who seems to know every dish on the menu inside out. Their confidence in explaining the specials, answering questions about ingredients, and making recommendations is noticeable.

This is the power of staff training. It empowers your team with the knowledge and skills necessary to provide a top-tier dining experience.

Research has shown that trained staff can significantly impact customer satisfaction. Here are some interesting statistics:

> *"63% of diners seek out small, independent restaurants over national chains… [and] 47% of customers prefer to spend their money in an "employee-centric" restaurant."*[2]
>
> Fit Small Business

Your staff becomes the face of your brand, and their ability to confidently navigate the menu, accommodate special requests and ensure a smooth dining experience directly affects customer perception and loyalty.

The sad reality, though, is that many small restaurant owners overlook this critical aspect. Despite guest satisfaction being at the heart of the hospitality industry, up to 70% of restaurant workers never get customer service training.[3]

---

2. Fit Small Business, "45 Key Restaurant Industry Statistics for 2023", https://fitsmallbusiness.com/restaurant-statistics/

3. Opentable, *"Restaurant training in 2023: A comprehensive overview for owners"* https://restaurant.opentable.com/resources/restaurant-training/

An exceptional dining experience isn't confined to the four walls of your restaurant; it lingers in the minds of your guests long after they've paid the bill. Well-trained staff play a pivotal role in creating these memorable moments.

Training Helps Meet Higher Customer Expectations

In today's restaurant landscape, customers are more sophisticated than ever before. They're well-informed, often relying on online reviews and social media recommendations before choosing a dining destination.

Before even setting foot in your establishment, many customers engage in a ritual of pre-dining research. They scour online reviews, browse through mouthwatering Instagram photos, and seek recommendations from friends and family.

According to data from TripAdvisor, a staggering *"94% of U.S. diners say online reviews influence their dining decisions."*[4] And, *"89% of dining research is done by mobile before visiting a restaurant,"* according to Google.[5] This means that even before guests arrive, they already have certain expectations.

When guests walk through your restaurant's doors, their first interaction is generally with your staff. This initial contact sets the tone for the entire dining experience.

Your staff is not just there to serve food; they are there to create a dining experience. Customers expect more than just an order-taking and

---

4. TripAdvisor, *"Influences on Diner Decision-Making"*, https://www.tripadvisor.com/ForRestaurants/r3227

5. Google, *"Restaurant Study"*, https://www.thinkwithgoogle.com/consumer-insights/consumer-trends/mobile-dining-research-statistics/

meal-delivering robot. They want your staff to guide them through the culinary journey, offering insights, recommendations, and solutions to any inquiries or concerns.

The training of your staff plays a pivotal role in ensuring they can meet these expectations. They should be well-versed in the menu, capable of describing dishes in enticing detail, and adept at accommodating dietary preferences or restrictions. Their ability to navigate the fine line between attentive service and intrusive hovering is essential.

Each positive interaction between your staff and a guest is a building block of customer satisfaction. It reinforces the idea that your restaurant not only meets but surpasses expectations. Every interaction counts in an era where customer feedback travels at the speed of light.

Training Helps Ensure Consistency

Consistency is the linchpin of any successful restaurant. It's what transforms a one-time visitor into a loyal patron. Whether you run a small cafe or a bustling full-service restaurant, your customers expect the same level of quality and service every time they walk through your doors. When your staff is trained properly, every guest experiences the same level of service.

Proper training is about imparting skills, knowledge, and behaviors that align with your restaurant's vision. When your staff understands and embodies these principles, they become the guardians of your restaurant's reputation.

One way to achieve this consistency is by implementing standardized procedures. These procedures cover everything from setting tables, taking orders, handling guest complaints, and presenting the bill. When your staff follows these procedures diligently, it helps ensure a smooth experience.

Consistency isn't just about meeting expectations; it's about building trust and a stellar reputation. When customers know they can rely on your restaurant to deliver exceptional experiences, they become advocates for your brand.

Think of every positive dining experience as a building block in the foundation of your restaurant's reputation. These experiences are shared with friends, family, and online communities. Word-of-mouth recommendations, bolstered by consistent service, can be a powerful driver of customer traffic.

In essence, staff training is the vehicle that drives consistency in your restaurant. It ensures that your staff understands and upholds the standards and procedures that define your brand. Consistency should not be taken lightly; it's a necessity for long-term success.

Creating a Positive Workplace Culture

The dining experience you offer to your customers is not just crafted in the kitchen but also woven together by your staff's attitude, dedication, and camaraderie. As you're no doubt aware, the entire restaurant industry has been facing profound staffing challenges since the COVID-19 pandemic. Nurturing a positive workplace culture retains talented team members and contributes to the overall success of your establishment.

In this section, we'll examine strategies and techniques to cultivate a workplace culture that fosters unity, encourages innovation, and sustains your team's motivation. We'll look at the role of leadership in shaping this culture, the art of team building, and the tangible benefits it brings to your restaurant.

The High Cost of Turnover

Before we dive into staff retention, let's address the elephant in the room: the cost of turnover.

> *"According to the National Restaurant Association, the average restaurant loses $150,000 in a year due to staff turnover. Additionally, the Center for Hospitality Research at Cornell University estimates that losing a front-line employee costs an employer an average of $5,864."*[6]

Now, consider the impact on your bottom line if you have to replace multiple employees every few months.

Turnover doesn't just drain your financial resources; it disrupts the continuity of service. Frequent staff changes can result in inconsistencies in customer experience, leading to dissatisfaction and a tarnished reputation.

Benefits of Staff Retention

On the flip side, staff retention brings stability and several significant benefits. Loyal, experienced team members become familiar faces to your customers. They develop relationships, remember preferences, and contribute to a warm and inviting atmosphere. Industry research has shown that an increase in employee retention can lead to a corresponding increase in customer satisfaction.

> *"[E]ach one-star improvement in a company's Glassdoor rating corresponds to a 1.3-point out of 100 improvement in customer satisfaction scores — a statistically significant impact,*

---

6. QSRSoft, *"The Cost of Turnover in Quick Service Restaurants"*, https://www.qsrsoft.com/blog/the-cost-of-turnover-in-quick-service-restaurants-plus-steps-to-reduce-employee-turnover/

> which was more than twice as large in industries where employees interact closely and frequently with customers."[7]

Happy, long-term staff members tend to provide more consistent and personalized service, which directly impacts customer loyalty.

So, this begs the question—how can you improve staff retention in your restaurant?

- **Invest in Training:** Adequate training not only equips your staff with essential skills but also makes them feel valued and invested.

- **Recognition and Rewards:** Implement recognition programs to acknowledge and reward exceptional performance. A simple *"Employee of the Month"* program can go a long way.

- **Clear Career Paths:** Provide opportunities for career advancement within your establishment. When staff can see a future, they are more likely to stay.

- **Work-Life Balance:** Encourage a healthy work-life balance. Overworked and stressed staff are more likely to seek employment elsewhere.

- **Open Communication:** Foster an environment where staff can voice concerns, offer suggestions, and feel heard.

By focusing on staff retention, you not only reduce turnover costs but also create a loyal, motivated team that's committed to your restaurant's success. With the right strategies, you can build a team that stays and thrives,

---

7. Harvard Business Review, *"The Key to Happy Customers? Happy Employees"*, https://hbr.org/2019/08/the-key-to-happy-customers-happy-employees

contributing to a positive workplace culture that defines your restaurant's identity.

Leadership's Role in Creating a Positive Culture

Your approach to leadership shapes the culture of your restaurant, and it plays a pivotal role in reducing staff turnover while fostering a positive workplace culture.

Research from Gallup highlights the connection between leadership and workplace culture. It suggests that leaders who focus on their employees' strengths and well-being are more likely to create engaged and motivated teams. These teams, in turn, are more likely to stay loyal to their organization.

> *"When employees feel that their company cares and encourages them to make the most of their strengths, they are more likely to respond with increased discretionary effort, a stronger work ethic, and more enthusiasm and commitment."*[8]
>
> Gallup

Whether you choose to take credit for it or not, your restaurant's culture reflects your leadership style. It's the atmosphere that envelops your establishment, influencing how your team interacts, communicates, and collaborates. A positive workplace culture doesn't happen by accident; it's crafted by the actions and attitudes of leaders like you.

---

8. Gallup, *"How Employees' Strengths Make Your Company Stronger"*, https://www.gallup.com/workplace/231605/employees-strengths-company-stronger.aspx

Your actions as a leader speak louder than words. When you demonstrate respect, empathy, and professionalism, your team is more likely to follow suit. Conversely, if you exhibit negative behaviors or a lack of appreciation for your staff, it can erode morale and drive turnover. Leading by example sets the tone for your restaurant's culture.

Open and transparent communication is a cornerstone of effective leadership. Regularly engaging with your staff, seeking their input, and providing constructive feedback creates an environment where everyone feels valued and heard.

Your staff can provide a veritable treasure trove of insights about the health of your restaurant's operations. By actively listening and implementing their suggestions when feasible, you not only boost their morale but also contribute to a culture of innovation and continuous improvement.

Recognizing and developing your staff is another critical aspect of leadership. When employees feel acknowledged and have growth opportunities, they are more likely to stay. Consider implementing reward programs for outstanding performance and provide clear paths for advancement. These efforts motivate your team and contribute to a sense of belonging and loyalty.

Diversity can also be a powerful asset. A diverse team brings a range of perspectives and ideas to the table, fostering creativity and innovation. However, to harness the full potential of diversity, it's essential to create an environment where every staff member feels valued and heard.

For example, conduct staff meetings that encourage open discussions and idea-sharing from team members with varied backgrounds and experiences. This diversity of thought can lead to breakthrough solutions and contribute to a more vibrant workplace culture.

Leadership is the compass that steers your restaurant's culture. It's a driving force in reducing staff turnover and creating a positive workplace environment. By leading with integrity, fostering open communication, and investing in your team's growth, you can shape a workplace culture that not only retains talent but also propels your restaurant toward success.

Staff's Impact on Table Turnover

As we've gone over the 5 table turnover mistakes, you may have noticed that for each one, staff played a vital role. In this section, we're going to build on that concept a bit more and discuss some additional ways that your staff contributes to an effective table turnover rate.

Why Timing Is Everything

Imagine a group of guests walking into your restaurant, greeted by a friendly hostess. They are promptly seated, and their drink orders are taken within minutes. As they peruse the menu, their server arrives with a warm smile, ready to assist with any questions. The courses flow smoothly, and when the meal concludes, the bill is presented promptly without rushing the diners.

This is the art of timing in restaurant service, and your staff's mastery of it is pivotal in achieving optimal table turnover rates.

Effective table turnover ensures that each dining party has ample time to savor their meal, engage in conversation, and enjoy the overall experience without feeling rushed. At the same time, it requires a level of efficiency that allows you to accommodate the next reservation or walk-in promptly. Your staff's ability to gauge and manage this timing is crucial.

Your staff's understanding of the flow of your restaurant—from taking orders to delivering dishes and clearing tables—impacts the overall timing and flow. This ensures that no part of the process becomes a bottleneck.

The art of timing isn't just about speed; it's also about attentiveness. Your staff should be attuned to the needs of each table, recognizing when guests require assistance or when they prefer a more leisurely pace. The balance between attentiveness and respect for the guest's pace is a skill that can significantly influence their satisfaction and the likelihood of a return visit.

Finally, the transitions between dining parties are crucial for effective table turnover. Your staff's ability to clear tables efficiently, reset them for the next guests, and ensure a smooth handoff between shifts or sections is vital.

The art of timing in restaurant service is a multifaceted skill that your staff must master. It's not just about speed but also about attentiveness and respect for each guest's dining pace. When executed effectively, it not only enhances the dining experience but also optimizes your table turnover rate, contributing to the success of your restaurant.

Balancing Efficiency with Guest Experience

Attentive service is the hallmark of a memorable dining experience. It involves your staff's ability to cater to the unique needs of each table, creating an atmosphere where guests feel valued and cared for. Yet, it's equally about ensuring that this personalized service does not compromise the efficiency required for effective table turnover.

Successful servers take a few extra moments to engage with guests beyond the mere exchange of pleasantries. They inquire about special occasions, dietary preferences, or even favorite flavors. This subtle approach to building rapport not only enhances the guest's experience but also enables your staff to tailor their service effectively.

> *"Among the most important things diners say they want restaurants to know (and remember) their names (65 percent) and favorite drink (50 percent)."*[9]
>
> OpenTable

---

9. Benbria, "*10 Stats On The Importance of Customer Experience In Restaurants*", https://benbria.com/importance-of-cx-restaurants/

Your staff's ability to remember a regular's favorite dish or a guest's dietary restrictions is an invaluable asset in creating loyal patrons. One of the true hallmarks of attentive service is their ability to anticipate guest needs even before they're voiced.

This anticipation comes from your staff's keen observation and familiarity with the flow of the dining experience. When done skillfully, it not only enhances the guest's satisfaction but also speeds up service without feeling rushed.

Communication and Adaptation

Attentive service also hinges on clear and efficient communication among your team. When kitchen staff communicates seamlessly with servers, it ensures that orders are prepared promptly. Likewise, when the front-of-house team coordinates effectively, it ensures that each guest's needs are met without disruptions.

Effective communication minimizes bottlenecks and ensures a smooth flow of service. It prevents avoidable delays that can impact table turnover rates while maintaining the high standards of a memorable dining experience.

Lastly, the art of attentive service involves listening to guest feedback and adapting accordingly. Feedback provides insights into areas where your staff can fine-tune their service to better meet guest expectations. Restaurants grow when they take guest comments seriously, address concerns, and make improvements based on suggestions.

> *"38% of all customer complaints are on social media and review sites. Restaurants get only 14% of all complaints."* [10]

---

10. Benbria, "*10 Stats On The Importance of Customer Experience In Restaurants*", https://benbria.com/importance-of-cx-restaurants/

The art of attentive service is a vital component of effective table turnover. Your staff's ability to balance efficiency with personalized, anticipatory service not only optimizes turnover rates but also creates an atmosphere where guests want to return—knowing they'll be treated to a dining experience that's both efficient and memorable.

Staff's Impact on Profitability

There's a common phrase among restaurant owners: *"Your staff is your greatest asset."* This isn't just a platitude; it's a simple truth. In this section, we explore the pivotal role your staff plays in shaping your restaurant's profitability.

Now, up to this point, we've explored the intricate web of staff training, workplace culture, leadership, and the art of service. Now, it's time to connect the dots and understand how these elements directly correlate with your restaurant's bottom line.

Your staff isn't just responsible for delivering dishes to tables; they are the frontline ambassadors of your brand, the driving force behind guest satisfaction, and, ultimately, the key to your restaurant's long-term success. Their actions, attitude, and dedication can differentiate a thriving establishment from one struggling to stay afloat.

The Power of Efficiency

Efficiency is the backbone of a profitable restaurant. It's about ensuring that every aspect of your operation, from kitchen workflows to front-of-house service, maximizes output while minimizing waste.

Staff training should extend beyond delivering exceptional service to your restaurant's operations. They should understand how to prioritize tasks, manage customer expectations, and work together cohesively. Well-trained employees are less likely to make errors, leading to fewer wasted resources, lower food costs, and improved guest satisfaction.

A critical component of efficiency is time management. Efficient time management directly impacts table turnover rates, allowing you to accommodate more guests during peak hours.

Moreover, time management extends to the kitchen, where the timing of dishes can significantly enhance the guest experience. When each individual order arrives at the table at the right moment, it not only improves satisfaction but also contributes to efficient table turnover.

Efficiency also plays a role in minimizing waste. When a kitchen manages inventory effectively, ingredients are used before they spoil. Efficient portion control by staff also prevents over-serving, which can also lead to excessive food waste and increased costs.

A keen focus on reducing waste not only boosts profitability but also aligns with sustainability practices, which are becoming increasingly important to environmentally-conscious diners.

Finally, efficiency is closely linked to cost control. When staff members are diligent in managing portions, minimizing waste, and adhering to cost-conscious practices, your restaurant's expenses are kept in check.

A diligent focus on operational efficiency is a powerful tool in enhancing your restaurant's profitability. Your staff's training, time management, and cost-consciousness are all integral to this initiative. By investing in staff training and promoting an efficiency-focused culture, you're not just running a restaurant; you're running a business poised for long-term success.

Customer Loyalty: The Lifeline of Profitability

One of the key goals of your restaurant is to ensure that guests return not just out of habit but out of genuine loyalty. When they eagerly recommend your establishment to friends and family, their repeat visits become a steady stream of revenue. This is the power of customer loyalty—a force that can significantly impact the profitability of your restaurant.

Your staff's ability to create experiences that meet and exceed guest expectations is critical in convincing new guests to choose your restaurant over competitors. This is critical, given the cost of acquiring new customers far exceeds that of retaining existing ones; customer loyalty is paramount to profitability.

Your staff's commitment to delivering exceptional service directly influences guest satisfaction and loyalty. It's not simply about meeting basic expectations; it's about consistently exceeding them. When guests feel a personal connection with your brand, they are more likely to return and become loyal patrons.

Now, admittedly, things don't always go smoothly. So, exceptional service is also about how your staff handles challenges. When a guest encounters an issue, and your staff resolves it promptly and professionally, this can turn a potentially negative experience into one that strengthens customer loyalty.

Encouraging guest feedback and using it to drive continuous improvement is another aspect of fostering customer loyalty. Your restaurant should actively seek input from guests, value their opinions, and implement changes based on their suggestions. This not only enhances the guest experience but also showcases your commitment to meeting their needs.

Customer loyalty isn't a passive outcome but a result of your staff's commitment to exceptional service, personal connections, problem resolution, and continuous improvement.

When guests become loyal supporters of your restaurant, they not only contribute to its profitability through repeat business but also serve as a valuable marketing source, attracting new customers through word-of-mouth recommendations.

Let's move on to brand advocacy.

Turning Guests into Brand Advocates

Closely coupled with customer loyalty is the ultimate goal of turning one-time customers into brand advocates. To be sure, the keys to a profitable restaurant are marketing, advertising, and promotion. However, one of the most potent forms of promotion is from the mouths of your own diners. When your staff's dedication goes above and beyond expectations, this has the power to transform one-time visitors into enthusiastic advocates.

The mindset of providing exceptional service doesn't just focus on the present; it's about creating loyal brand ambassadors. Imagine a guest leaving your restaurant smiling, eager to share their experience with friends and family. These word-of-mouth recommendations are a testament to the power of exceptional service in building your restaurant's reputation.

Your staff plays a pivotal role in crafting these memories. Their commitment to ensuring that every guest leaves not just satisfied but delighted is what transforms your restaurant into a go-to destination. When your staff delivers experiences that transcend the ordinary, it helps to cultivate a loyal customer base, turning guests into enthusiastic advocates who return time and again and convince others to do the same.

Reputation Management: The Guardian of Profitability

Your restaurant's reputation is a fragile yet formidable asset. It's not merely about what happens within your four walls; it extends to the perception of your brand in the eyes of the public. This reputation can be a powerful magnet, drawing in new customers and retaining loyal ones.

"72% of consumers say that positive reviews make them trust a local business more." [11]

Bloom Intelligence

Your restaurant's online presence is an integral part of reputation management. Make no mistake – guests search for your restaurant online first. You want them to find a website that is informative, up-to-date, and visually appealing. They should also find positive reviews and engaging social media content that reflects a vibrant and well-managed establishment.

"According to Upserve, 90% of guests research a restaurant online before dining—more than any other business type in their study. And, 57% of those guests viewed restaurant websites before selecting where to dine." [12]

Bloom Intelligence

Your staff's commitment to delivering a reliable and outstanding experience is pivotal in shaping your restaurant's reputation. Consistently great service creates a sense of trust. When guests know they can rely on your restaurant to meet or exceed their expectations, they are more likely to return and recommend your establishment to others.

PRO TIP: If you encourage customers to post and tag your restaurant on social media, be sure to prominently display the profile information on your menu and other conspicuous places in your restaurant. Having a QR code that links to your dominant social media profile allows for a faster upload process.

At times, reputation management also involves crisis management. There may be situations where an unforeseen issue arises—a food safety concern, a negative news story, or a public relations challenge. Your staff's ability to handle these situations with professionalism and a commitment to rectify the issue can mitigate damage to your reputation.

PRO TIP: If the issue involves possible or pending litigation, make sure that your staff is instructed to follow the non-disclosure instructions from your legal team. This may involve not speaking directly to the press about certain matters. Always ensure that legal protocols are adhered to — especially in a crisis.

Engaging with the community is another aspect of reputation management. This happens when your restaurant actively participates in local events, supports charitable causes, and fosters a sense of community. Your staff can play a role in these efforts, creating a positive image that resonates with potential customers.

Reputation management doesn't happen by accident; it's an ongoing commitment that involves your staff at every level. Your team's dedication to delivering consistent service, maintaining a positive online presence, and effectively managing crises can safeguard and enhance your restaurant's reputation, ultimately contributing to its profitability.

Continuous Training and Development

The restaurant landscape is ever-evolving. So, stagnation is not an option. Success lies in hiring and training competent staff and nurturing a culture of continuous learning and development within your restaurant.

Your staff, from front-line servers to seasoned chefs, must adapt to changing customer preferences, industry trends, and new technologies. Continuous training and development are how you ensure that your team remains not just relevant but also excels in an increasingly competitive market.

This section is about more than just theoretical concepts. It's about tangible results. When your staff is equipped with the tools to excel, your restaurant reaps the benefits. From increased efficiency and reduced turnover to elevated guest satisfaction and profitability, the impact is far-reaching.

Fostering a Culture of Continuous Learning

The restaurant industry thrives on innovation and must constantly adapt to changing tastes and preferences. Therefore, continuous training is not merely a choice; it's a necessity. The competitive edge your restaurant gains through ongoing learning ensures that your staff can deliver exceptional service and is adept at handling new challenges.

Continuous training isn't only about skill development; it's also about investing in your staff's career growth and job satisfaction. When staff members feel valued and supported, they are more likely to stay with your restaurant, reducing turnover costs and maintaining a stable, experienced team.

Ongoing training is also an essential element in boosting guest satisfaction. When guests notice the depth of knowledge in your staff's recommendations or the flawless execution of their dishes, these positive guest experiences often translate into loyalty and repeat business.

The key to success in continuous training is creating a culture of learning within your restaurant. It's about creating an environment where your staff is encouraged to seek out growth, share knowledge with their peers, and embrace new challenges as opportunities rather than daunting obstacles.

Your commitment to continuous training and development will empower your staff to enhance their skills, gain job satisfaction, and ultimately contribute to guest satisfaction and loyalty. It's an investment that pays dividends.

The ROI of Employee Development

Investing in the growth and development of your staff is an investment in the future of your restaurant. Studies have consistently shown that organizations that prioritize employee development experience higher productivity, increased employee satisfaction, and lower turnover rates.

Employee development also creates a robust leadership pipeline within your restaurant. Imagine a manager who started as a server or a head chef who once manned the line. Internal promotions are a testament to your commitment to nurturing talent from within.

A happy staff is a productive staff. When employees see a clear path for career advancement, receive regular training, and know that their personal development matters to the organization, this boosts satisfaction and retention.

Finally, employee development ensures that your restaurant remains adaptable and innovative. Continuous learning equips your staff to embrace new culinary trends, technologies, and customer preferences, positioning your restaurant as a leader rather than a follower.

While many small restaurants view employee development as an expense, it's really a strategic investment with a high return. It enriches your staff's skillset, creates a talent pipeline, enhances employee satisfaction, boosts guest loyalty, and helps ensure your restaurant's ability to thrive in an ever-changing industry.

Let's wrap up our discussion with a few key takeaways from the chapter.

Key Takeaways

In the restaurant world, think of exceptional service as the *"golden key"* that unlocks customer loyalty and profitability. In this chapter, we discussed the pivotal role staff training plays in delivering memorable experiences, cultivating a positive workplace culture, and boosting table turnover rates.

We've explored the power of customer loyalty, understanding that it's not just about repeat visits but also increased spending and invaluable word-of-mouth marketing. Your staff's dedication to exceptional service is the linchpin that converts casual diners into lifelong patrons.

Moreover, creating a positive workplace culture is not an afterthought; it's a strategic directive. When your team is motivated, engaged, and feels like an integral part of your restaurant's success, their enthusiasm spills over into their interactions with guests, elevating the overall dining experience.

Furthermore, we explored how your staff contributes to effective table turnover rates. From greeting guests with a warm smile to managing orders efficiently, their actions impact the pace at which tables become available for new guests, directly influencing your restaurant's profitability.

Understanding how staff can influence table turnover and profits is essential for streamlining operations and maximizing revenue potential. It's a win-win relationship where your staff's efficiency and commitment directly correlate with your restaurant's success.

Finally, we discussed the critical aspects of fostering a culture of continuous learning within your restaurant. Ongoing training and development aren't just buzzwords; they are your means to adapt, grow, and remain competitive in a dynamic industry.

Investing in employee development isn't merely a financial expenditure—it's an investment in your restaurant's future. It enriches your staff's skills, fosters loyalty, enhances guest satisfaction, and ensures your restaurant can innovate and adapt.

As you reflect on these insights, remember that the long-term success of your restaurant hinges on your commitment to staff training and customer service excellence. These aren't separate entities but interconnected components of a thriving establishment.

Let's move on to our next chapter, where we start to explore the role of technology.

CHAPTER 10
Embracing Technology for Long-Term Success

"What new technology does is create new opportunities to do a job that customers want done."

Tim O'Reilly

The rapid explosion of technology over the past 30 years has reshaped every aspect of our lives. In today's dynamic and competitive business environment, staying ahead of the curve is a necessity. The success of a restaurant is no longer solely determined by the quality of its food and service but also by its ability to embrace and integrate technology effectively.

In this ever-evolving landscape, where customer expectations are shaped by rapidly advancing technology, restaurant owners face the critical task of leveraging digital solutions to enhance their operations and, more importantly, to avoid costly mistakes that could hinder table turnover and profitability.

From the moment a customer enters your establishment until they leave, your adoption of technology plays a pivotal role in shaping their perception of your restaurant. It can enhance efficiency, streamline customer interactions, and influence your restaurant's online reputation.

This chapter will explore technology's pivotal role in modern restaurant operations. We will explore why you must embrace technology, from enhancing efficiency and customer experience to reducing costs and adapting to shifting consumer behaviors.

Finally, we will lay the groundwork for the next chapter, which will examine some practical steps for selecting and integrating the right technology solutions to help ensure the long-term success of your restaurant.

The Role of Technology in Restaurant Operations

Technology plays a critical role in balancing traditional culinary artistry with the ever-evolving expectations of diners. It should be considered as a catalyst for transformation, redefining how modern restaurants operate.

In an era where gaining attention is becoming increasingly difficult, time is of the essence, and competition is fierce. Technology offers solutions that empower restaurant owners to thrive. From enhancing operational efficiency to creating unforgettable customer experiences, embracing technology can open doors to new possibilities.

Enhancing Efficiency and Customer Experience

Efficiency isn't just about moving faster; it's about optimizing for better results. Technology offers practical solutions that can fine-tune your restaurant's operations. From order management systems that streamline kitchen communication to automated inventory tracking that prevents shortages, technology's contribution to boosting efficiency is undeniable.

On the flip side, customer experience is the heart and soul of your restaurant. It encompasses every touchpoint your guests have with your brand.

Technology can elevate these experiences, making them memorable, convenient, and enjoyable. From digital reservations and contactless payment options to personalized recommendations, technology empowers you to create moments that keep diners coming back.

Technology's Impact on Operational Efficiency

The pursuit of efficiency is a never-ending journey. Every task, every process, and every moment counts, and this is where technology can become your trusted ally. In this section, we will explore some transformative ways in which technology streamlines restaurant operations.

Technology has the remarkable ability to optimize operations, reducing the margin for error and increasing the pace of service.

Here are some ways that it accomplishes this.

- **Automated Order Management Systems:** The heart of any restaurant, the kitchen, can be a whirlwind of activity during peak hours. Order management systems can electronically transmit orders from the front of the house to the kitchen, reducing the chances of miscommunication and errors. This streamlined process ensures that dishes are prepared efficiently and in the order they are received, leading to quicker table turnover and satisfied customers.

- **Inventory and Supply Chain Management:** Maintaining an accurate inventory is essential for cost control and ensuring that you always have crucial ingredients. Technology solutions offer real-time tracking and automated alerts when supplies are running low. This not only prevents disruptions but also helps in reducing food waste, positively impacting your bottom line.

- **Reservation and Seating Management:** Technology has revolutionized how reservations are made, and tables are allocated. Advanced reservation systems allow customers to book tables online, reducing the need for manual reservation management. Furthermore, these systems can optimize seating arrangements, ensuring every table is occupied efficiently throughout service hours.

- **Staff Scheduling and Time Management:** Effectively managing your workforce is pivotal in achieving operational efficiency. Software tools help create optimized staff schedules and match labor costs to customer demand. This prevents overstaffing and ensures you have the correct number of hands on deck when needed.

- **Contactless Payments:** Speed and convenience are paramount. Contactless payment options enable customers to settle their bills swiftly, reducing waiting times at the cashier. This not only improves table turnover but also enhances the overall dining experience.

Incorporating these technological solutions into your restaurant operations can significantly impact efficiency and your bottom line. It's not only about keeping up with the times; it's about outwitting the competition and remaining profitable.

Technology's Impact on Customer Service

Delivering exceptional customer service is a key focus area of your restaurant. Yet, as technology evolves, the rules of the game have also evolved. Here are some ways that technology aids in the quest to provide outstanding customer experiences:

- **Personalized Dining Experiences:** Picture this: A diner walks into your establishment, and the server already knows their dietary preferences and favorite dishes. This level of personalization is made possible by Customer Relationship Management (CRM) systems that store and retrieve customer data, allowing you to tailor their unique dining experience. These personal touches not only impress customers but also foster loyalty.

- **Tableside Ordering Devices:** Say goodbye to the traditional pad and paper. With tableside ordering devices, waitstaff can take orders directly from customers, sending them straight to the kitchen, thereby reducing the margin for error. This speeds up service and ensures that diners get precisely what they ordered.

- **Digital Feedback and Surveys:** Instant feedback is a goldmine for improvement. With digital feedback systems, customers can share their thoughts and suggestions instantly. This real-time information can guide you in making necessary adjustments, thereby enhancing the overall dining experience.

- **Waitlist and Reservation Apps:** Avoiding frustratingly long wait times is paramount to customer satisfaction. With waitlist and reservation apps, customers can join a virtual queue or book a table remotely, minimizing the time spent waiting. This convenience leaves a positive impression on patrons.

- **Digital Loyalty Programs:** Rewarding repeat customers is a time-tested strategy, and technology has breathed new life into loyalty programs. Digital loyalty cards, apps, and reward systems incentivize return visits and gather valuable customer data for better targeting.

- **Streamlined Payment Options:** Fumbling for cash or waiting for the bill can irritate both parties. Contactless payment options, such as mobile wallets and payment apps, streamline the payment process, allowing customers to settle their bills quickly and efficiently.

By embracing these technological solutions, you can not only streamline your restaurant's operations but also create a dining experience that is seamless, personalized, and memorable. Your patrons will appreciate the efficiency and convenience that technology brings to the table.

Remaining Competitive in the Digital Age

Our modern world has ushered in a new era of dining, where customer expectations are shaped by convenience and innovation. Today, it's not enough to rely solely on the traditional pillars of restaurant success (i.e., great food). Instead, you now must leverage the power of technology to elevate your game and meet the ever-rising standards of customers.

Let's explore technology's pivotal role in keeping your restaurant relevant and at the forefront of your customer's minds. Here, we will unravel the compelling reasons why embracing technology is not merely a choice but a strategic imperative for any restaurant that aspires to remain competitive.

The Ever-Evolving Expectations of Diners

Today, information and immersive experiences are literally at our fingertips. As a result, diners' expectations have undergone a profound transformation. It's crucial to recognize that the modern diner arrives at your doorstep with a set of expectations influenced (albeit sometimes unrealistically) by the digital world.

Here are a few insights into what today's diners are looking for and how technology can help you meet those demands.

- **Immediate Gratification:** In an era of instant messaging and same-day deliveries, patience is a virtue that's rapidly eroding. Modern diners expect prompt service and quick access to information. They don't want to wait for menus, orders, or payments. Technology can bridge this gap by offering solutions like QR code menus and contactless payments, ensuring a swift and seamless dining experience.

- **Customization and Personalization:** The era of one-size-fits-all dining experiences is dying out. Modern diners want personalized interactions and tailored recommendations. They want their preferences to be remembered and honored. Customer Relationship Management (CRM) systems and data-driven insights enable you to offer a more personalized service, enhancing customer loyalty and satisfaction.

- **Seamless Booking and Reservations:** Booking a table should be as easy as booking on a ridesharing app. Modern diners prefer the convenience of digital reservation systems that allow them to reserve a table with a few taps on their smartphones. Integrating these systems meets their expectations and optimizes table turnover and capacity management.

- **Transparency and Authenticity:** In an era of online reviews and social media, transparency and authenticity are highly valued. Diners want to know where their food comes from, its nutritional information, and the story behind it. Utilizing technology, you can share this information through your website and social media, building trust and engaging diners on a deeper emotional level.

- **Connectivity:** Modern diners are constantly connected even while dining out. They expect reliable Wi-Fi and may want social media-friendly moments to share with their network. Offering Free high-speed Wi-Fi connectivity can enhance the overall dining experience.

PRO TIP: It may be a wise choice to separate the network that your business relies on (e.g., point-of-sale machines and internal accounting systems) from the Wi-Fi network shared by diners. Nefarious people are everywhere, and it is critical to ensure business continuity.

We'll take a more detailed look at this in another section, but for now, know that these evolving expectations reflect the profound impact of the digital age on the restaurant industry. To stay competitive, it's imperative to not only understand but also adapt to these shifts.

Technology isn't just a bunch of fancy tools and gadgets; it's the conduit through which you can meet and exceed the expectations of the modern diner. This not only secures customer loyalty but also ensures that your restaurant remains relevant and competitive in the digital age.

Other Ways That Technology Gives Your Restaurant an Edge

Following the COVID-19 pandemic, the restaurant industry has become even more competitive. In this new economic reality, gaining an edge can mean the difference between thriving and merely scraping by. Technology can be a game-changer that can provide your restaurant with a definitive edge over the competition.

Here are some ways:

- **Enhanced Customer Engagement:** Engaging diners beyond the dining table is essential for building lasting relationships. Email marketing campaigns, loyalty programs, and social media platforms allow you to stay connected with your customers, even when they're not dining with you. This ongoing interaction can boost customer loyalty and keep your restaurant top-of-mind.

- **Efficient Inventory Management:** Maintaining the right ingredients in the right quantities is pivotal in both cost control and offering a consistent dining experience. Inventory management software helps you optimize stock levels, reduce waste, and ensure that popular dishes are always available.

- **Data-Driven Decision-Making:** In the digital age, data is king. Technology tools allow you to gather and analyze data on customer preferences, dining habits, and spending patterns. This invaluable insight can inform menu changes, pricing strategies, and marketing campaigns, allowing you to make informed decisions that resonate with your target audience.

- **Streamlined Operations:** From kitchen operations to front-of-house management, technology helps streamline processes and reduces the risk of human error. Modern POS systems, for instance, improve order accuracy, speed up service, and facilitate staff management.

- **Online Ordering and Delivery:** The rise of food delivery services is a testament to the changing dining habits of consumers. Cross-platform tools empower you to tap into this lucrative market by integrating online ordering and delivery platforms. This expands your customer base and caters to the growing demand for convenience.

- **Enhanced Marketing and Branding:** Technology offers powerful tools for marketing and branding. From eye-catching websites to social media campaigns, you can craft a compelling digital presence that attracts and retains customers.

- **Competitive Insights:** Keeping an eye on the competition is crucial for staying in the game. Tools such as social listening platforms let you monitor the strategies and performance of rival restaurants, allowing you to adjust your approach accordingly.

Incorporating these technological advantages into your restaurant's operations is a strategic move that can provide a tangible edge in an industry where every advantage matters.

Reducing Cost and Increasing Profit Margins

Your restaurant's financial health is not only determined by what you earn but also by how efficiently you manage your costs. In this section, we will discuss reducing expenses and optimizing your profit margins—two pillars that can make or break your restaurant's success.

Technology plays a pivotal role in profitability. From streamlining operations to automating processes, it offers a variety of solutions that can help you financially. It's not only about saving money; it's about investing in the right technology to maximize your profitability while maintaining the quality and integrity of the overall dining experience.

How Technology Can Help Cut Expenses

The pursuit of financial efficiency is a continuous journey. Every dollar saved is a dollar that contributes to your restaurant's profitability. Here are some ways that technology can be a powerful mechanism for trimming expenses and bolstering your bottom line:

- **Streamlined Inventory Management:** Manually managing inventory is time-consuming and prone to errors. Inventory management software automates the tracking and replenishing of stock. By reducing overstocking, minimizing wastage, and ensuring that ingredients are always on hand, you can significantly cut food costs.

- **Efficient Staff Scheduling:** Overstaffing can quickly erode profit margins, while understaffing can compromise service quality. Workforce management software uses data-driven insights to optimize staff schedules. This means you're only paying for labor when you truly need it, aligning staffing costs with customer demand.

- **Energy Management Systems:** Energy costs are a substantial expense. Modern energy management systems use sensors and automation to optimize heating, cooling, and lighting, reducing energy consumption and expenses.

- **Digital Payment and Billing:** ATM machines are becoming harder to find. Embracing digital payment options, such as mobile wallets and contactless payments, expedites the payment process.

- **Food Waste Reduction:** Food waste is both an environmental concern and a financial drain. Technology can help you track and reduce waste by analyzing consumption patterns, suggesting portion sizes, and finding creative ways to repurpose ingredients.

- **Point of Sale (POS) Systems:** Modern POS systems collect data on sales, customer preferences, and inventory in real-time. This data can inform decisions that optimize pricing, menu offerings, and sales strategies to maximize profitability.

These tools are your financial allies in the quest for cost reduction. By strategically implementing technology in these areas, you cut expenses and lay the foundation for a leaner, more profitable restaurant operation.

Boosting Profitability Through Tech Integration

Profitability isn't just about cutting costs; it's also about optimizing revenue.

Here's how technology integration can elevate your restaurant's profitability.

- **Menu Engineering:** Your menu isn't just a list of dishes; it's a strategic revenue driver. Modern technology tools can provide insights into customer preferences and buying patterns, helping you design a menu that maximizes profits. You can increase the average check size by strategically pricing items, highlighting high-margin dishes, and adjusting offerings based on seasonality.

- **Online Ordering and Delivery Platforms:** The world of dining has expanded beyond your restaurant's walls. Online ordering and delivery platforms enable you to tap into a broader customer base and generate additional revenue streams. Integrating with popular delivery platforms allows you to reach customers who prefer the convenience of dining at home.

- **Reservation Systems:** Efficiently managing table reservations ensures that every seat is optimized for revenue. Modern reservation systems help you allocate tables effectively, minimize no-shows, and reduce idle seating. This results in higher table turnover and increased revenue.

- **Upselling and Cross-Selling:** Technology can be your silent salesperson. POS systems equipped with suggestive selling prompts can encourage servers to upsell and cross-sell complementary items, which enhances their dining experience while boosting revenue.

- **Loyalty Programs:** Loyalty programs and apps encourage repeat visits and increased spending from loyal customers. Offering rewards, discounts, and exclusive deals through these programs can drive higher revenue from a dedicated customer base.

- **Data-Driven Decision Making:** Technology helps you collect and analyze data on customer behavior and preferences. This data-driven insight enables you to make informed decisions about menu changes, pricing strategies, and marketing campaigns, all aimed at increasing profitability.

By strategically integrating technology across these facets of your restaurant, you're enhancing the dining experience and maximizing your establishment's financial potential. Profitability is about boosting revenue while delivering exceptional value to your customers.

Key Takeaways

The ability to leverage technology effectively can mean the difference between success and mediocrity. In this chapter, we explored the critical role technology plays in your restaurant, offering valuable insights and strategies.

Technology is truly the backbone of modern restaurant operations – streamlining processes, enhancing customer experiences, and boosting profitability. As a small restaurant owner, you need to understand that technology is an essential asset for staying competitive in today's digital age.

Okay, now that we've discussed the importance of implementing technology solutions, let's discuss how actually to go about it.

This will be the subject of the next chapter.

CHAPTER 11
Implementing Technology Solutions in Your Restaurant

"Technology gives us power, but it does not and cannot tell us how to use that power. Thanks to technology, we can instantly communicate across the world, but it still doesn't help us know what to say."

Jonathan Sacks

When implemented correctly, technology solutions can revolutionize your restaurant, from order management and reservations to how you engage with your customers. In this chapter, we'll explore the practical aspects of selecting and implementing technology solutions that align with your restaurant's unique needs and goals.

As we go through this chapter, remember that technology should not be viewed as a disruption but as a valuable tool that can empower your restaurant to thrive in an ever-evolving industry.

Let's start with the first step – assessing your restaurant's needs.

Assessing Your Restaurant's Needs

Before grabbing your checkbook, having a clear understanding of your unique requirements and objectives is essential. In this section, we'll explore the crucial first step: evaluating your restaurant's specific needs and challenges.

Technology should never be adopted blindly. Instead, it should be a strategic choice tailored to address your restaurant's specific pain points and opportunities. Regardless of your restaurant's operating model, the right technology solutions can enhance efficiency, improve customer experiences, and boost your bottom line.

Identify Areas Where Technology Can Make the Most Impact

First, it's crucial to identify the areas where a given technology solution can make the most significant impact. This strategic assessment will serve as the foundation for selecting the tools that align with your restaurant's unique needs and goals.

Here's how you can pinpoint those areas where technology can be a game-changer:

- **Streamlining Order Management:** One of the most apparent areas where technology can enhance efficiency is order management. Consider how technology can optimize the process of taking and fulfilling orders, reduce errors, and speed up the flow of dishes from the kitchen to the table.

- **Inventory and Supply Chain Management:** Technology can revolutionize how you manage inventory and supplies. Automation can help you track stock levels, predict demand, and optimize ordering, reducing waste and lowering costs.

- **Reservations and Table Turnover:** If your restaurant experiences high demand, technology can improve reservations and table turnover. Evaluate whether a digital reservation system or table management software could help you maximize your seating capacity.

- **Customer Experience Enhancement:** Technology can significantly impact the dining experience. Think about how digital menus, interactive ordering systems, or loyalty programs can enhance customer flow while encouraging repeat business.

- **Marketing and Promotion:** Assess how technology can support your marketing efforts. Email marketing platforms, social media management tools, and customer relationship management (CRM) systems can help you reach and engage with your target audience effectively.

- **Payment and Billing:** Explore technology options for seamless and secure payment processing. Contactless payment methods, mobile wallets, and integrated point of sale (POS) systems can simplify transactions for both staff and customers.

- **Staff Training and Management:** Consider how technology can assist with staff training and management. Learning management systems (LMS) and employee scheduling software can improve training efficiency and optimize staffing levels.

- **Data Analytics and Insights:** Leverage technology to gain valuable insights into your restaurant's overall performance. Analytics tools can help you track key metrics, such as sales trends, customer preferences, and operational efficiencies.

- **Growth and Scalability:** If you have ambitions for growth, assess how technology can support your expansion plans. Scalability should be a consideration in selecting technology solutions.

Remember that every restaurant is unique, and what works for one may not work for another. Tailor your technology investments to align with your specific needs and priorities. Conduct surveys, gather feedback from staff and customers, and analyze your operational processes to pinpoint areas where technology can drive meaningful improvements.

Create a Technology Roadmap for Your Restaurant

Now that you've identified the areas where technology can have the most impact on your restaurant, it's time to create a technology roadmap. Think of this roadmap as part of your overall strategic plan for your restaurant's success.

Here's how to create one:

- **Define Your Objectives:** Start by clarifying your restaurant's overarching objectives. What do you aim to achieve with technology integration? Whether it's improving efficiency, enhancing the customer experience, increasing revenue, or all of the above, your objectives will guide your technology choices.

- **Prioritize Areas of Improvement:** Based on your needs assessment, prioritize the areas where technology can make the most significant difference. Determine which solutions will have the most immediate impact on your goals.

- **Set a Budget:** Establish a budget for your technology investments. Consider both the initial costs and ongoing expenses, such as maintenance and subscription fees. Ensure that your budget aligns with your restaurant's financial capabilities.

PRO TIP: Sometimes, technology costs can spiral out of control if you're not careful. Ensure that you have enough money in your budget for unexpected expenses like technology upgrades, integration, or hiring consultants when needed.

- **Research Technology Solutions**: Research and identify specific technology solutions that address your prioritized areas of improvement. Look for reputable vendors and systems that offer the features and support you need.

PRO TIP: Salesmen will often promise the world but fall short when an issue arises. Get recommendations from other restaurant owners. Ask about integration with your current system and have the sales staff demonstrate any integration points among systems. Ensure that tech support is included with any software or system(s) you purchase. The company should stand by their work and offer phone, email, chat, and on-site support if needed.

- **Evaluate Integration:** Consider how your chosen technology solutions will integrate with your existing systems. Seamless integration is crucial to avoid disruptions in your restaurant's operations.

- **Create a Timeline:** Develop a timeline for implementing each technology solution. Consider factors such as installation, training, and testing phases. Ensure the timeline is realistic and accounts for potential technology issues or setbacks.

- **Training and Onboarding:** Plan for training and onboarding your staff on the new technology. Adequate training ensures your team can use the systems effectively and maximize the benefits.

 **PRO TIP:** If possible, negotiate including staff training as a perk of buying a new system. This step can save you time and money by showing you and your staff how to operate the equipment or software.

- **Test and Refine:** Before full-scale implementation, thoroughly test the technology solutions. Identify and address any issues or concerns. Refine your implementation plan based on the test results.

- **Monitor Progress:** Once the technology is in use, establish a system for monitoring its effectiveness. Track key performance metrics to gauge how well the technology is helping you achieve your objectives.

- **Adapt and Evolve:** Technology is ever-evolving, and so should your technology roadmap. Stay informed about new advancements and be ready to adapt your plan to incorporate innovations that can further benefit your restaurant.

Remember that your technology roadmap is a dynamic document that should evolve alongside your restaurant's needs and goals. Regularly revisit and adjust it as necessary to ensure that your technology investments continue to support your success.

Point-of-Sale (POS) Systems

I wanted to kickoff our discussion of implementation with a Point-of-Sale (POS) system.

Why?

Because your Point-of-Sale (POS) system is the heart of your operations. It's the central hub where orders are placed, payments are processed, and critical data is collected. In this section, we'll discuss selecting and implementing the right system for your establishment.

POS systems have come a long way from simple cash registers. Today's advanced systems are powerful tools that can transform your restaurant's efficiency, accuracy, and profitability. Whether you're a new restaurant owner searching for your first POS system or an experienced operator looking to upgrade, understanding this technology is crucial.

Some Benefits of Modern POS Systems

Today, modern Point of Sale (POS) systems offer numerous benefits that can boost your restaurant's success. In this section, we'll explore some of the advantages of adopting a modern POS system and why it's a cornerstone of efficient and profitable restaurant management.

- **Streamlined Order Management:** Modern POS systems excel in order accuracy and speed. They enable your staff to take orders efficiently, customize them to customer preferences, and transmit them seamlessly to the kitchen. This minimizes errors and ensures that dishes are prepared and served promptly.

- **Enhanced Customer Experience:** With intuitive interfaces and features like digital menus and mobile ordering, modern POS systems contribute to an improved dining experience. They let customers place orders conveniently and even split bills, all while reducing wait times.

- **Real-time Inventory Tracking:** Inventory management is another core feature of modern POS systems. They allow you to monitor stock levels in real-time, automate reordering processes, and minimize food wastage. This results in cost savings and improved profitability.

- **Comprehensive Reporting and Analytics:** Access to robust reporting and analytics is another feature of modern POS systems. They provide insights into sales trends, customer preferences, and employee performance. Armed with this data, you can make informed decisions to optimize your menu, pricing, and operations.

- **Integration Capabilities:** Most modern POS systems can integrate with other technology solutions, such as reservation systems and delivery platforms. This creates a unified ecosystem that simplifies operations and enhances the overall dining experience.

- **Employee Efficiency:** POS systems reduce the burden on your staff. They automate routine tasks like order calculations and payment processing, allowing your team to focus on providing excellent service and improving table turnover.

- **Scalability:** Modern POS systems can scale to meet your needs, whether you operate a small restaurant or a multi-location chain. They can accommodate a growing number of terminals and handle increased order volumes without compromising performance.

- **Cost Efficiency:** While the initial investment in a modern POS system may seem substantial, it often leads to long-term cost savings. Improved efficiency, reduced errors, and better inventory management also contribute to lower operating costs and higher profit margins.

- **Customer Data Utilization:** Modern POS systems collect valuable customer data, including order history and contact information. This data can be leveraged for personalized marketing campaigns and loyalty programs, fostering customer retention and repeat business.

By embracing a modern POS system, you're not just adopting a tool; you're really investing in your restaurant's success. These systems are designed to optimize restaurant management, helping to drive profitability while providing a memorable dining experience.

How to Choose the Right POS System

Selecting the right Point of Sale (POS) system for your restaurant is a pivotal decision that can significantly impact your business's efficiency and success. To make an informed choice, you'll need to navigate a sea of options, each offering unique features and capabilities. Let's look at a few essential steps to choose a POS system that aligns with your restaurant's specific needs.

- **Define Your Requirements:** Begin by understanding your restaurant's unique requirements. Consider factors such as your menu complexity, order volume, and the type of cuisine you serve. Are you a small cafe or a full-service fine-dining establishment? Your POS system should cater to your restaurant's specific demands.

- **Determine Your Budget:** Establish a clear budget for your POS system. Costs can vary widely, from affordable tablet-based systems to high-end, feature-rich solutions. Be sure to factor in not only the initial purchase cost but also ongoing fees like software updates and support.

- **Identify Must-have Features:** Make a list of must-have features. These could include menu customization, table management, split-check capabilities, and integration with other software, such as reservation systems or accounting tools. Prioritize these features based on their importance to your restaurant's operations.

- **Research Reputable Providers:** Look for reputable POS system providers. Read reviews, seek recommendations from fellow restaurateurs, and check online forums. Focus on vendors known for reliability, customer support, and industry-specific expertise.

- **Consider Hardware:** Decide on the type of hardware that suits your restaurant. This includes terminals, tablets, and even handheld devices. Consider factors like durability, ease of use, and how they fit into your restaurant's layout.

PRO TIP: If using handheld devices, make sure they can withstand moisture, heat, cold, impact from being dropped, etc. Handheld devices often accompany staff into the kitchen, in the freezer, outside for curbside orders, and in other places. Make sure your equipment can handle these extremes.

- **Ensure Compatibility:** Ensure that the POS system you choose is compatible with your existing infrastructure. This includes compatibility with your payment processors, printers, and any other hardware or software you currently use.

PRO TIP: Your technology should work for you – not the other way around. This cannot be overemphasized. When compatibility issues arise, they can be costly and time-consuming. Make sure that all of your systems work together seamlessly. Also, remember that software is dynamic. POS and other systems are constantly being patched and updated. Ensure your systems work following each software update by performing a quick "dry run" before you open for the day.

- **Test the User Interface:** User-friendliness is crucial. Test the user interface to ensure it's intuitive and easy for your staff to navigate.

Complex systems can lead to errors and slow down service, so simplicity is key.

- **Explore Integration Options:** Integration capabilities can streamline your operations. Check whether the POS system can integrate with your reservation system, accounting software, and other third-party applications you rely on.

 **PRO TIP:** When integrating systems, ensure role-based access on both platforms. This means that you can set up and control who has access to what. For example, you wouldn't want a server to have access to your accounting system.

- **Evaluate Support and Training:** Assess the level of support and training offered by the POS provider. Adequate training is essential to ensure that your staff can maximize the system's potential. Reliable support is crucial for addressing any issues that may arise.

- **Check for Scalability:** Consider your restaurant's growth potential. Choose a system that can scale with your business, accommodating additional terminals or locations as needed.

- **Read the Fine Print:** Before finalizing your choice, carefully read the contract and understand the terms and conditions, including fees, warranties, and support agreements. Don't hesitate to seek clarification on any points you find confusing.

- **Seek References:** If possible, ask the POS provider for references from other restaurant owners who have implemented their system. Hearing about their experiences and successes can provide valuable insights.

 **PRO TIP:** If the vendor provides references, be sure to follow up with them. First, do a little reconnaissance and order a meal there to see how smooth their operation really is. Then, schedule a formal meeting to get honest, insightful feedback on the points mentioned above.

Choosing the right POS system is an investment in your restaurant's future. Take your time, do your due diligence, and involve key members of your team in the decision-making process. Remember that the ideal POS system is one that not only meets your current needs but also adapts to your restaurant's evolving requirements, ensuring efficient operations for years to come.

Training Staff on POS Usage

Once you've selected the Point of Sale (POS) system for your restaurant, you need to ensure that your staff can use it effectively. Proper training is essential to harness the full potential of your POS system and avoid common pitfalls. In this section, we'll look at training your restaurant staff to use the POS system efficiently.

- **Plan Comprehensive Training:** Start by planning a comprehensive training program. It should cover all aspects of POS usage, from taking orders to processing payments, and include any specialized features relevant to your restaurant.

- **Train All Staff:** Ensure that all relevant staff members receive training. This includes servers, bartenders, kitchen staff, and managers. Consistency in training is vital for smooth operations.

- **Customize Training:** Tailor your training to the roles of your staff. Front-of-house staff may need more extensive training on order entry and customer interactions, while back-of-house staff might focus on order preparation and inventory management.

- **Use Hands-on Training:** Practical, hands-on training is incredibly effective. Let your staff interact with the POS system and practice various tasks. Encourage questions and immediate feedback.

- **Develop Training Materials:** Create training materials, including user manuals and quick-reference guides. These materials can serve as valuable references for your staff as they become more familiar with the system.

PRO TIP: Leverage any online training available from the POS vendor. Many times, they will have comprehensive onboarding and training programs online that your staff can take on their own time. If hard copies of training materials are needed, request these from the vendor. They will often give them to you for free or for a nominal printing cost.

- **Regularly Schedule Training Sessions:** Depending on staff turnover rates and system updates, periodic refresher training may be necessary. Schedule training sessions as needed to keep your team up to date.

- **Don't Forget Data Security:** Train your staff on the importance of data security. Ensure they understand the proper handling of customer information and payment data to maintain compliance with industry standards.

- **Encourage Basic Troubleshooting Skills:** Teach your staff basic troubleshooting and problem-solving skills. They should be able to handle minor issues and know when to seek assistance for more complex problems.

- **Foster Confidence:** Building confidence in your staff is essential. Encourage them to embrace the system and assure them that mistakes are part of the learning process. A confident team is more likely to use the system to its fullest potential.

- **Provide Ongoing Support:** Offer ongoing support for your staff. Have a designated point person available to address questions or issues that arise during service.

- **Seek Feedback:** Encourage feedback from your staff regarding the POS system. Their input can help identify areas for improvement and additional training needs.

- **Monitor Usage:** Keep an eye on how your staff is using the POS system during service. Regularly review transactions and reports to ensure correct usage and identify any potential training gaps.

Effective training is an investment that pays off in streamlined operations, reduced errors, and improved customer service. By providing your staff with the skills and confidence to navigate your POS system, you empower them to deliver exceptional dining experiences, boosting both customer satisfaction and your restaurant's bottom line.

Remember, a well-trained team is one of your restaurant's most valuable assets.

In the next section, we'll examine QR Codes and Virtual Menus.

QR Codes and Virtual Menus

Throughout the restaurant industry, the use of QR Codes and Virtual Menus has generally been slow to gain adoption. Many small restaurant owners simply don't grasp how powerful these tools are. Technology has reshaped the way restaurants can engage with their customers, and one notable innovation is the integration of QR codes and virtual menus.

In this section, we'll take a deep dive into QR codes and virtual menus, exploring their significance and benefits and how to effectively incorporate them into your restaurant's operations. QR codes and virtual menus hold amazing potential to enhance efficiency, elevate the customer experience, and adapt to modern diners' evolving needs and preferences.

The Convenience of Digital Menus

Picture this scenario: Your customers enter your restaurant, take their seats, and reach for their smartphones. With a quick scan of a QR code displayed on the table, they instantly access your entire menu, with vivid images and detailed descriptions. There is no need to wait for a physical menu to arrive; the dining experience has already begun.

This scenario illustrates how the power and convenience of digital menus are transforming diner engagement. In this section, we'll look at some additional ways digital menus enhance the dining experience and streamline restaurant operations.

- **Instant Access to Information:** Digital menus put your restaurant's offerings at your customers' fingertips. With a simple scan or tap, they can view your menu, including specials, prices, and dietary information, creating a sense of control and convenience.

- **Rich Visuals:** Digital menus allow you to showcase your dishes with high-quality images. Studies show that visual representations of food can stimulate appetite and influence diners' choices, ultimately boosting sales.

- **Real-time Updates:** Menu changes are much easier with digital menus. Whether you're adding seasonal dishes, updating prices, or displaying daily specials, these changes can be made instantly and without the need for costly and time-consuming menu reprinting.

- **Contactless Ordering:** In an age of health and safety concerns following the COVID-19 pandemic, contactless options have become an integral part of the dining experience. Digital menus eliminate the need for physical menus that pass through multiple hands, providing a safer dining experience.

- **Upselling Opportunities:** Digital menus can incorporate upselling prompts. By strategically placing recommendations or add-on options, you can increase the average check size without putting pressure on your staff.

- **Improved Order Accuracy:** With customers entering their orders directly into the system, the likelihood of errors due to miscommunication or illegible handwriting is significantly reduced, leading to higher order accuracy.

- **Multilingual Support:** For restaurants in diverse areas or tourist destinations, digital menus can offer multilingual support, ensuring that all patrons can easily understand the menu and make informed choices.

- **Enhanced Customer Engagement:** Digital menus can include interactive elements, such as links to chef profiles, behind-the-scenes videos, or customer reviews. These features can enrich the overall dining experience and keep customers engaged.

- **Environmental Sustainability:** By reducing the need for printed menus, digital menus contribute to environmental sustainability by saving paper and reducing waste.

- **Data Insights:** Digital menus can collect valuable data on customer preferences and order trends. This data can inform menu optimization, marketing strategies, and customer relationship management.

Incorporating digital menus into your restaurant not only meets the demands of modern diners but also offers practical benefits that can positively impact your bottom line. With digital menus, you can provide a more convenient and engaging dining experience while also adapting to the changing landscape of restaurant operations.

As you consider the integration of digital menus into your restaurant, remember that the key to success lies not only in the technology itself but also in effectively implementing this valuable tool.

Implementing QR Codes and Virtual Menu Solutions

Now it's time to explore how to go about implementing QR Codes and Virtual Menus in your restaurant. Here are some practical guidelines:

- **Choose a Reliable QR Code Generator:** Begin by selecting a trustworthy QR code generator tool. Many online services allow you to create QR codes for free. Ensure that it generates QR codes that integrate with your virtual menu platform.

- **Design and Print QR Codes:** Create visually appealing QR codes that incorporate your restaurant's branding. These codes will be displayed on tables, menus, and promotional materials.

- **Select a Virtual Menu Platform:** Research and choose a virtual menu platform that aligns with your restaurant's needs and budget. Consider factors such as user-friendliness, customization options, and compatibility with your Point of Sale (POS) system.

- **Upload Your Menu:** Use the chosen virtual menu platform to upload your restaurant's menu. Ensure that it's clear, concise, and visually appealing, with high-quality images and informative descriptions.

- **Generate QR Codes for Tables:** Create unique QR codes for each table in your restaurant. These codes will link directly to the digital menu corresponding to that table. Print and display them prominently for easy customer access.

- **Train Your Staff:** Familiarize your staff with the QR code and virtual menu system. They should be able to assist customers with any questions and troubleshoot common issues.

- **Promote the Digital Experience:** Let your customers know about the new digital menu options. Use table tents, signage, and social media to inform them about the convenience and safety of the digital menu experience.

- **Monitor Usage and Gather Feedback:** Keep an eye on how customers are engaging with the digital menus. Collect feedback from both staff and patrons to identify areas for improvement.

- **Ensure Compatibility with Your POS System:** Ensure your POS system is compatible with your chosen virtual menu platform. Integration between the two systems helps to streamline operations.

- **Regularly Update Your Digital Menus:** Keep your digital menus up to date with the latest offerings, prices, and promotions. Regular updates ensure that customers always have access to accurate information.

- **Address Technical Issues Promptly:** Have a plan in place to address any technical issues that may arise, such as connectivity problems or software glitches. Prompt resolution is crucial to maintaining a smooth dining experience.

By following these steps, you'll be well on your way to providing your customers with a modern, contactless dining experience that enhances their convenience and safety while streamlining your restaurant's operations.

3rd Party Reservation Systems

The ability to efficiently manage reservations is a cornerstone of your restaurant's success. In this section, we will explore the significance of 3rd party reservation systems, the benefits they bring to your restaurant, and the steps to successfully integrate them into your operations.

The days of juggling multiple phone calls, hurriedly scribbled reservations, and the occasional mix-up are long gone. With 3rd party reservation systems, restaurants have gained the ability to streamline their booking processes, optimize table turnover, and offer customers a more seamless and convenient reservation experience.

Streamlining the Reservation Process

Managing high demand was a logistical challenge in the past, but not anymore. Thanks to modern 3rd party reservation systems, your restaurant can streamline the reservation process, making it a win-win for both you and your diners.

In this section, we will explore the power of 3rd party reservation systems, focusing on how they change the way you manage bookings and enhance the overall dining experience for your customers.

- **Simplified Reservation Management:** 3rd party reservation systems provide you with a centralized platform to manage all your reservations. No more scribbled notes, missed calls, or double-booked tables. With a few clicks, you can see your restaurant's reservations at a glance, making it easier to plan and optimize table assignments.

- **Real-time Availability:** These systems allow you to display real-time table availability to customers. When someone wants to book a table, they can instantly see which time slots are open, reducing the back-and-forth that often comes with phone reservations.

- **Customer Convenience:** Convenience is key in the modern dining landscape. With 3rd party reservation systems, customers can book a table at your restaurant at their convenience, whether it's during office hours or late at night. This flexibility encourages more reservations and attracts a broader customer base.

- **Reduced No-Shows:** No-shows can be a headache, resulting in lost revenue and empty tables. Many 3rd party reservation systems offer automated confirmation and reminder features, significantly reducing the likelihood of no-shows.

- **Waitlist Management:** These systems often include waitlist management features. When your restaurant is fully booked, customers can join a waitlist, and you can notify them when a table becomes available, enhancing customer satisfaction.

- **Data Insights:** Reservation systems gather valuable data on booking patterns, customer preferences, and peak dining hours. This data can help guide your marketing strategies, menu offerings, and staffing decisions.

- **Integration Capabilities:** Some reservation systems seamlessly integrate with your Point of Sale (POS) system, making it easier to manage reservations, track guest preferences, and streamline billing.

- **Enhanced Customer Experience:** The convenience of online reservations and the elimination of booking errors contribute to an improved customer experience. It's a hassle-free process that sets a positive tone for their dining experience.

- **Increased Efficiency:** By automating many aspects of reservation management, you can allocate your staff's time more efficiently. Hosts and hostesses can focus on welcoming and serving customers rather than answering phones and managing reservations manually.

With these benefits in mind, it's clear that 3rd party reservation systems have become an indispensable tool for modern restaurants. By streamlining the reservation process, you not only save time and reduce errors but also enhance the overall dining experience, making it a win-win for your restaurant and your customers.

How to Integrate Third-Party Reservation Platforms

Let's dive into the nitty-gritty details of how to integrate these platforms into your restaurant's operations. Here are some practical suggestions to help guide you through the process:

- **Choose the Right Reservation Platform**: The first step is to carefully select a 3rd party reservation platform that aligns with your restaurant's needs. Consider factors like cost, features, and the platform's reputation in the industry.

- **Set Up Your Account**: Once you've made your choice, sign up and create an account with the reservation platform. You'll need to provide essential information about your restaurant, including contact details, hours of operation, and table availability.

- **Customize Your Profile**: Personalize your profile to make it appealing to potential diners. Upload high-quality images of your restaurant, menu, and special dishes or offerings. A visually appealing profile can attract more customers.

- **Configure Reservation Settings**: Fine-tune your reservation settings to match your restaurant's capacity and operational hours. Specify the number of covers you can accommodate per time slot and any restrictions on group sizes.

- **Integrate with Your Website**: Be sure to integrate your reservation platform with your restaurant website. Be sure that it is displayed prominently on the home page. Provide a user-friendly interface that allows visitors to book tables directly from your site.

- **Train Your Staff**: Ensure that your staff is well-versed in using the reservation system. They should understand how to confirm bookings, handle walk-ins, and manage the waitlist efficiently.

- **Promote the Reservation Option**: Let your customers know that they can now make reservations through the new platform. Use your website, social media, and in-house marketing materials to spread the word.

- **Monitor and Manage Reservations**: Regularly check the reservations coming in and adjust your staffing and table arrangements accordingly. Make sure to keep track of any special requests or notes from diners.

- **Confirm and Remind**: Many reservation platforms offer automated confirmation and reminder features. Use these features to reduce the likelihood of no-shows.

- **Analyze Data and Feedback**: Review the data provided by the platform. Analyze reservation trends, customer preferences, and feedback to make data-driven decisions for your restaurant.

- **Evaluate Performance**: Periodically assess the performance of your chosen reservation platform. Is it meeting your expectations? Are there any glitches or issues that need attention? Consider soliciting feedback from staff and customers.

- **Stay Up-to-Date**: Keep your reservation platform up-to-date with accurate information regarding your restaurant's menu, pricing, and operating hours. Timely updates ensure that customers have access to the latest details.

By following these steps, you'll successfully integrate 3rd party reservation platforms into your restaurant's operations. This modern approach not only streamlines the booking process but also enhances the overall dining experience for your customers.

Now, let's move on to delivery platform integration.

Delivery Platform Integration

Delivery platform integration has become an essential component of restaurant technology that allows you to expand your reach and cater to a broader audience. In this section, we'll explore the ins and outs of integrating your restaurant with popular delivery platforms, unlocking new avenues for growth and customer engagement.

The dining scene has evolved over the past five years (from about 2018 to 2022). So have the expectations of your patrons. The majority of customers now want the convenience of enjoying restaurant-quality meals in the comfort of their homes or offices. This shift in consumer behavior has given rise to a booming food delivery industry, and you have the opportunity to capitalize on this trend.

The Rise of Food Delivery Platforms and Services

Picture this: A busy professional, swamped with work, wants to enjoy a delicious restaurant meal without leaving the office. A family, exhausted after a long day, craves their favorite dishes from a local restaurant but prefers to dine in the comfort of their home while watching a movie.

In both scenarios, food delivery services come to the rescue, reshaping the restaurant industry in the process.

In recent years, the food delivery landscape has undergone a significant transformation. What was once an expensive, niche service has evolved into a multi-billion-dollar industry with an ever-expanding customer base.

Here are some key reasons why.

- **Skyrocketing Demand**: The demand for food delivery services has surged, driven by changing consumer preferences and a desire for convenience.

"The revenue in the Online Food Delivery market is forecasted to reach US$1.02tn in 2023." [1]

Statisa

- **Evolving Consumer Behavior**: Today's diners increasingly value ordering restaurant-quality meals and having them delivered to their doorstep. This shift in consumer behavior has made adopting food delivery platforms a necessity for many restaurants to survive and compete.

- **Expanding Delivery Ecosystem**: Food delivery platforms like Uber Eats, DoorDash, Grubhub, and Postmates have established themselves as key players in the industry, offering extensive reach and convenience to customers.

- **COVID-19 Acceleration**: The COVID-19 pandemic accelerated the adoption of food delivery services, as dining restrictions and safety concerns prompted more people to order food for delivery or takeout.

- **Opportunity for Restaurants**: For restaurant owners, integrating with these delivery platforms presents a significant opportunity to tap into a vast and diverse customer base without the need for additional brick-and-mortar locations.

- **Diverse Cuisine Options**: Delivery platforms have made it easier for diners to explore a wide variety of cuisines from various

---

1. Statista, *"Online Food Delivery – Worldwide"*, https://www.statista.com/outlook/dmo/online-food-delivery/worldwide

restaurants, expanding their culinary horizons.

- **Customer Loyalty**: Restaurants that offer delivery through these platforms can build customer loyalty, as customers can conveniently reorder their favorite dishes with a few taps on their smartphones.

- **Competitive Advantage**: In a competitive restaurant landscape, providing food delivery services can set your establishment apart from others and attract a broader audience.

- **Revenue Boost**: Delivery orders can significantly boost a restaurant's revenue, especially during peak dining hours or busy weekends.

- **Data Insights**: Integrating with food delivery platforms provides access to valuable data on customer preferences, order patterns, and sales trends, which can guide your restaurant's short-term and long-term strategies.

Understanding the rise of food delivery services is just the beginning. Let's explore how to effectively integrate your restaurant with these platforms, allowing you to leverage their potential to enhance customer satisfaction, increase revenue, and keep pace with the evolving demands of today's diners.

How to Integrate Delivery Platforms

While the specific nuances of each delivery platform vary, here are some general steps to integrate your restaurant with these platforms.

- **Choose the Right Delivery Platforms**: Begin by selecting the most suitable delivery platforms for your restaurant. Consider factors like their reach, customer base, and fees. It's often beneficial to start with one or two platforms and expand as needed.

- **Create Your Restaurant Profile**: Sign up and create a comprehensive profile for your restaurant on each selected platform. Provide detailed information about your menu, pricing, hours of operation, and delivery zones. High-quality images of your dishes can entice potential customers.

PRO TIP: Invest in professional photography when selecting and uploading images. Modern smartphones may take great pictures, but they also may fall short. Blurry images, poor lighting, or unappetizing dishes will cause you to lose sales. Remember, high-quality, professional photos can be used on multiple platforms, on your print menu, and on your website. Spend the money and have it done right.

- **Menu Optimization**: Tailor your menu for delivery. Some dishes may not travel well, so consider offering a curated menu that maintains the quality of your food during transit.

PRO TIP: Consider the climate of your local area. For instance, Sushi may not be an ideal candidate for delivery in Arizona, and a piping hot dinner may get cold in Chicago during winter. Invest in weather-appropriate packaging, and consider travel distance.

- **Pricing and Fees**: Determine your pricing strategy for delivery orders. Be transparent about any additional fees for delivery or service. Pricing should be competitive and reflect the value of your offerings. Don't undercharge.

- **Synchronize Your POS System**: To streamline order processing and avoid errors, integrate your Point of Sale (POS) system with the delivery platforms. This ensures that orders made through these platforms are automatically entered into your system.

- **Prepare Your Staff**: Train your kitchen and service staff to handle delivery orders efficiently. This includes packaging orders securely, adhering to delivery timeframes, and maintaining food quality standards.

- **Promote Delivery Services**: Spread the word about your new delivery partnership on your website, social media, and in-house marketing materials. Consider offering special promotions or discounts for first-time customers when appropriate.

- **Monitor Performance**: Regularly review your performance on the delivery platforms. Analyze order volumes, order details, customer feedback, and delivery times. Use this data to make adjustments and improvements.

- **Customer Feedback**: Encourage customers to leave reviews and feedback on the delivery platforms. Positive reviews can attract more customers, while constructive feedback helps you enhance your service.

- **Evaluate ROI**: Assess your delivery integration's return on investment (ROI). Track the revenue generated through these platforms, factoring in any associated costs. Evaluate whether it aligns with your business goals.

- **Expand Strategically**: Once you've mastered the integration process with one or two delivery platforms, consider expanding to additional platforms to reach a broader audience. Each platform may have its own unique customer base.

By following these steps, you'll be well on your way to seamlessly integrating your restaurant with food delivery platforms. Embracing this technology-driven strategy can help you not only meet the demands of today's diners but also position your restaurant for long-term success in an evolving industry.

Key Takeaways

As you reflect on our journey of integrating technology into your restaurant, it's essential to remember the transformative role it plays. This chapter has guided you through the strategic application of technology as an essential tool to elevate your restaurant's operations and customer experience.

Understanding your unique needs and objectives is the key to effective technology integration. It's not about adopting technology for the sake of being modern; it's about finding solutions that resonate with your restaurant's specific challenges and opportunities.

An important action item is the creation of a technology roadmap. This strategic plan should clearly align with your restaurant's goals and pave the way for successful technology integration. It involves setting objectives, prioritizing improvements, budgeting, and researching solutions that fit your unique context.

By focusing on specific technologies like Point-of-Sale (POS) systems, you'll better understand the central role technology plays in modernizing your restaurant. The right POS system can transform how orders are placed and processed, providing an improved experience for both staff and customers.

We also discussed the growing relevance of QR codes and virtual menus. This technology offers a contactless, engaging way for customers to interact with your menu, further enhancing the dining experience.

Additionally, integrating third-party reservation and delivery platforms has been highlighted as a crucial step in expanding your restaurant's reach and adapting to changing customer preferences. These platforms streamline operations and open up new avenues for customer engagement and revenue growth.

As you move forward in applying these insights, remember that technology in the restaurant industry is a dynamic, evolving landscape. Staying informed and adaptable, continually reassessing and refining your technology strategies, will be key to your long-term success.

CHAPTER 12
Social Media, Reputation Management, and Data Security

"It takes 20 years to build a reputation and five minutes to ruin it. If you think about that, you'll do things differently."
Warren Buffett

In this chapter, we'll cover a few miscellaneous technology-related topics you'll need to familiarize yourself with. Namely, the role that social media, reputation management, and data security play in your restaurant operations.

While these topics are not part of a single unified technology platform, I wanted to include them anyway because they are essential in keeping your restaurant running smoothly.

Let's start with Social Media and Online Reviews.

Social Media and Online Reviews

The old days when word-of-mouth recommendations were exchanged over fences or around dinner tables have evolved into a new era. Social media platforms and review websites have become the modern-day agora, where diners congregate to share their experiences, insights, and opinions.

The influence of social media and online reviews on the restaurant industry cannot be overstated. They can shape public perception, influence dining decisions, and drive foot traffic through your doors. A single tweet, a glowing review, or a captivating Instagram post has the potential to turn a casual browser into a loyal customer.

Building a Presence on Social Media

Remember that your restaurant's presence extends far beyond the physical walls of your dining space. It spans the digital universe, where social media platforms act as the modern-day town square, bustling with conversation, connection, and opportunity.

Social media platforms have transformed how diners discover, engage with, and share their restaurant experiences. Whether sharing a mouthwatering food photo on Instagram, posting a review on Yelp, or engaging in an X (Twitter) conversation about the latest culinary trends, these platforms have become the lifeblood of restaurant marketing.

PRO TIP: I'm going to go on a bit of a personal diatribe here before we get too deep into the subject. It is important to remember that social media is not a substitute for marketing your restaurant. Too many restaurant owners get caught up in *"likes," "followers,"* and emojis. They forget that the main point is to make money, not gain followers. Thus, they neglect their website, fail to engage with diners using email marketing, or even advertise their restaurant. Don't make this mistake.

Okay. Let's get back to the topic.

Here's how to build an impactful social media presence that keeps diners engaged and excited about your establishment.

- **Define Your Digital Persona**: Just as your restaurant has a unique personality, your online presence should reflect a distinct digital persona. Consider the tone, style, and voice that align with your brand and resonate with your target audience. Whether it's casual and friendly or upscale and refined, consistency is the key.

- **Choose the Right Platforms**: Not all social media platforms are created equal, and picking the ones that best suit your restaurant is crucial. For instance, Instagram is ideal for visually showcasing your dishes, while X (Twitter) can be a platform for timely updates and engaging with your audience.

- **Captivating Visuals:** In the world of social media, a picture is worth a thousand words. Invest in high-quality photography to showcase your food, ambiance, and staff. Eye-catching visuals can stop scrolling thumbs and prompt potential diners to learn more.

- **Content That Resonates**: Crafting content that resonates with your audience is vital to building engagement. Share behind-the-scenes glimpses, chef spotlights, and customer testimonials. Create a narrative that makes diners feel part of your restaurant's story.

- **Consistency Is Key**: Consistent posting keeps your audience engaged and your restaurant top of mind. Develop a content calendar that outlines when and what you'll post. It's not just about quantity; it's about delivering quality content regularly.

- **Interact and Respond**: Social media is a two-way street. Engage with your audience by responding promptly to comments, messages, and mentions. Encourage conversations and build relationships with your patrons online.

- **Use Analytics**: Don't rely on guesswork; use analytics tools provided by social media platforms to track the performance of your posts. Analyze which content resonates most with your audience and adjust your strategy accordingly.

Your online presence isn't just about posting pretty pictures; it's about creating a digital extension of your restaurant that captures the essence of your brand and resonates with your audience. It's a dynamic conversation, and by actively participating in it, you can craft a narrative that draws diners closer to your establishment.

Engaging with Your Audience

On social media platforms, engagement is the key that unlocks the door to a thriving online presence. It's about building authentic connections with your audience. Let's explore how to effectively engage with your online community, with the ultimate goal of transforming casual followers into loyal patrons.

- **Active Listening:** Social media is a bustling marketplace of ideas, opinions, and conversations. Make it a habit to actively listen to what your audience says about your restaurant and the broader dining scene. Monitor mentions, hashtags, and comments to stay attuned to their sentiments.

- **Prompt Responses:** Timeliness matters in the digital world. Respond to comments, questions, and messages promptly. Acknowledging and addressing customer inquiries or feedback swiftly demonstrates your commitment to customer service and fosters a sense of being heard.

- **Encourage User-Generated Content:** Encourage your patrons to share their experiences through user-generated content. Repost their photos, reviews, and stories on your social media channels, giving them a platform to shine. This not only boosts engagement but also builds a sense of community.

- **Storytelling:** Share stories that humanize your restaurant. Highlight your team members, their experiences, and their passion for creating each dish. Storytelling fosters a personal connection with your audience.

- **Run Contests and Giveaways:** Everyone loves a chance to win something. Hosting social media contests and giveaways can be an effective way to engage your audience. Encourage participation by tying contests to likes, shares, or user-generated content.

- **Use Emojis and Visuals:** Emojis and visuals can inject personality and emotion into your responses. Don't hesitate to use them when appropriate; they can convey warmth and enthusiasm in your interactions.

- **Address Negative Feedback Gracefully:** Negative feedback is inevitable, but how you handle it matters. Address criticism gracefully, empathetically, and professionally. Turn negative experiences into opportunities to showcase your commitment to improvement.

PRO TIP: Okay, another point I want to make here. If someone takes the time to follow your restaurant on social media, one of the most *BASIC* forms of common courtesy you can show is to follow them back. I have seen restaurants gain thousands of followers, and they'll follow a few people back. If you honestly don't have time to engage and follow back, then you should either hire someone or consider getting off the platform. When people see that you're not willing to engage with their content, they'll stop engaging with yours.

Engaging effectively with your audience on social media isn't just about promoting your restaurant; it's about building relationships, fostering loyalty, and creating a digital community that supports and celebrates your brand.

Okay. Let's move on to online reviews.

Online Reviews and Their Impact

Your restaurant's reputation is no longer confined to word-of-mouth discussions among friends and family. It now resides online, where every diner becomes a potential critic, and every rating and comment can sway the perceptions of countless others.

Online reviews are the currency of trust in the restaurant industry. In this section, we'll examine the impact that online reviews have on your restaurant's success and how you can leverage them to safeguard and enhance your restaurant's reputation.

First, know that the power of online reviews cannot be underestimated. They can make or break a restaurant's reputation, driving customers through your doors or sending them to your competitors.

For example, a potential customer is searching for a new restaurant to try. They reach for their smartphone, pull up a restaurant app, and begin scrolling through the options.

What's the first thing that grabs their attention?

More often than not, it's those little stars and snippets of feedback from fellow diners.

Customer reviews have evolved into the modern-day equivalent of word-of-mouth recommendations. They carry incredible weight in the minds of your diners.

Here's why they matter so much for your restaurant.

- **Decisions Shaped by Reviews:** Customer reviews directly influence dining decisions. Numerous studies have shown that consumers trust online reviews as much as they trust personal recommendations. When potential diners encounter positive reviews, it instills confidence in your restaurant.

"A study by BrightLocal revealed that a whopping 98% of consumers read online reviews to gauge the quality of a local business." [1]

BrightLocal

- **SEO and Visibility:** Beyond trust, customer reviews can impact your restaurant's online visibility. Search engines like Google consider review quantity and quality when ranking local businesses. Accumulating more positive reviews can elevate your search visibility, drawing more potential diners to your doorstep.

- **Constructive Feedback:** Even negative feedback can be a hidden gem. Constructive criticism can shine a light on areas that need improvement, allowing you to enhance your offerings and customer experience.

- **The Double-Edged Sword:** Here's the catch: the influence of customer reviews cuts both ways. Negative reviews, if not addressed appropriately, can deter potential diners, making their impact swift and lasting. Responding professionally and empathetically to negative feedback can help mitigate its effects.

- **Social Proof in Action:** People are wired to follow the crowd, and customer reviews provide just the social proof they crave. When potential diners see that others have relished their experi-

---

1. BrightLocal, *"Local Consumer Review Survey 2023"*, https://www.brightlocal.com/research/local-consumer-review-survey/

ences at your restaurant, it validates their decision to dine with you.

The key to mastering the power of customer reviews isn't about sitting back and waiting for feedback; it's about proactively nurturing a positive online reputation. Encourage satisfied diners to leave reviews, respond thoughtfully to their comments, and view feedback as a tool for continuous improvement.

Managing and Responding to Online Feedback

Your restaurant's reputation is molded by the dishes you serve and the opinions of those who dine with you. Every online review carries the potential to influence future diners.

Here are some tips for managing online feedback:

- **Be Responsive:** The digital world moves at a rapid pace, and so do online conversations about your restaurant. Responding promptly to customer reviews, both positive and negative, is essential. A swift response demonstrates your commitment to customer satisfaction and can help defuse potential issues.

- **The Professional Touch:** Craft your responses with professionalism and empathy. Acknowledge the customer's feedback, thank them for their input, and express your willingness to address any concerns. Remember that your response is a public statement that can influence the perceptions of others.

- **Turn Negatives into Positives:** Negative reviews can be disheartening but also present an opportunity. Instead of becoming defensive, use these reviews as a chance to showcase your dedication to improvement. Describe the steps you're taking to address the issue and invite the customer back for a better experience.

PRO TIP: Be solution-oriented by offering solutions or alternatives to the problem. Whether it's a refund, a complimentary meal, or a promise to improve a specific aspect of the dining experience, demonstrating your commitment to making things right can win back disgruntled customers.

- **Encourage Positive Engagement:** When you receive glowing reviews, express your gratitude. A simple "thank you" goes a long way in making customers feel appreciated. Encourage these patrons to become loyal advocates for your restaurant by sharing their positive experiences with others.

- **Seek Private Resolution:** Some issues are best resolved privately. If a customer encounters a problem requiring personal attention, contact them privately through direct messaging or email. This demonstrates your commitment to resolving their concerns.

- **Be Consistent:** Maintain consistency in your responses. Whether it's a positive or negative review, your tone and approach should reflect your restaurant's brand personality. Consistency builds trust and reinforces your restaurant's identity.

- **Monitor and Learn:** Monitor online reviews to identify recurring issues or patterns. Use this feedback as a learning tool to strategically improve your restaurant's operations, menu, or customer experience.

- **Get Professional Help:** As your restaurant's online presence grows, managing reviews can become significant. Consider using review management software or hiring professionals to monitor and respond to reviews effectively.

Managing and responding to online feedback is more than a simple courtesy; it's a strategic imperative. Each interaction is an opportunity to shape your restaurant's reputation, foster loyalty, and demonstrate your commitment to excellence.

Data Security and Compliance

Okay. Data Security and Compliance isn't the most fun topic and certainly isn't a page-turner, but in an age where technology is interconnected with restaurant operations, ensuring the security and compliance of your digital systems is paramount. One of the tradeoffs of the convenience and efficiency offered by Point of Sale (POS) systems, QR codes, virtual menus, and online reservations is the responsibility of safeguarding sensitive data.

You are entrusted with more data than you may realize, from customer payment information to employee records and essential business information. This data is critical to your restaurant's daily operations and valuable to cybercriminals seeking to exploit vulnerabilities in digital systems. In an era marked by data breaches and evolving regulations, it's necessary to take proactive steps to secure your restaurant's digital assets.

The Significance of Customer Data Protection

Today, data is as valuable as money. Therefore, safeguarding customer information is a non-negotiable responsibility for restaurant owners. Whether it's processing credit card transactions, managing reservation records, or simply retaining customer preferences, you are entrusted with sensitive data that must be protected with the utmost diligence.

Here are some reasons why protecting customer data is such a critical concern:

- **Trust and Reputation**: Customers entrust you with their personal and financial information when they dine at your restaurant or order online. Any breach of this trust can tarnish your restaurant's reputation irreparably.

- **Legal Obligations**: Various regulations, such as the Payment Card Industry Data Security Standard (PCI DSS) and the European Union's General Data Protection Regulation (GDPR), impose legal obligations on businesses to protect customer data.

- **Financial Impact**: Data breaches can result in substantial financial losses, from fines and legal fees to the cost of compensating affected customers.

- **Operational Disruption**: A data breach can disrupt your restaurant's operations, leading to downtime and lost revenue.

Basic Steps to Protect Customer Data

Now that you know the importance of customer data protection, here are some essential steps you should take:

- **Secure Your POS System**: Ensure your Point of Sale (POS) system is secure and compliant with industry standards. This includes encrypting payment data, regularly updating software, and restricting access to authorized personnel.

- **Employee Training**: Educate your staff about the importance of data security and their role in maintaining it. Train them to recognize and report potential security threats.

- **Data Encryption**: Ensure data encryption is present in transit and at rest. This adds an additional layer of security, making it difficult for unauthorized individuals to access sensitive information.

- **Access Control**: Restrict access to customer data to only those employees who require it for their job functions. Implement strong password policies and use multi-factor authentication where possible.

- **Regular Audits**: Conduct regular security audits and vulnerability assessments to identify and address potential weaknesses in your systems.

- **Incident Response Plan**: Develop an incident response plan that outlines steps to take in case of a data breach. This includes notifying affected customers and regulatory authorities promptly.

- **Compliance with Regulations**: Familiarize yourself with data protection regulations relevant to your restaurant's location and operations. Ensure your practices align with these regulations to avoid legal complications.

- **Third-Party Vendors**: If you use third-party vendors for services like payment processing or reservation management, ensure they also adhere to robust data security standards.

Consumer data protection is not a one-time effort but an ongoing commitment. As threats evolve, so too must your security measures. By following these steps and staying vigilant, you can significantly reduce the risk of data breaches and protect your customers' trust in your restaurant.

Data Privacy Regulations

Understanding and adhering to data privacy regulations is not a choice but a legal and ethical obligation for restaurant owners. Failing to comply with these regulations can lead to significant legal consequences and erosion of customer trust.

Data privacy regulations vary by country and region. Still, two key players often influence legislation worldwide: the European Union's General Data Protection Regulation (GDPR) and the U.S. Payment Card Industry Data Security Standard (PCI DSS).

GDPR: The GDPR sets stringent standards for protecting personal data and applies not only to European businesses but to any organization that processes the personal data of EU residents. Even if your restaurant is located outside of Europe, you are subject to the GDPR if you serve European customers.

PRO TIP: Don't dismiss the reach of the GDPR just because your restaurant isn't physically located the EU. There are a variety of scenarios that could potentially impact your restaurant. For example, if your U.S. restaurant sells T-shirts from your website to a customer in Canada, you may fall under the jurisdiction of these rules. As always, if you are in doubt, talk to a lawyer familiar with these regulations.

- **PCI DSS:** If your restaurant accepts credit card payments, the PCI DSS is a crucial set of security standards to adhere to. Non-compliance can result in fines and the loss of the ability to accept card payments.

These are just a few of the regulations that govern Data Privacy. There are others. Again, if in doubt, seek the guidance of a lawyer skilled in Data Privacy.

Tips to Ensure Compliance

Compliance with data privacy regulations is a multifaceted task.

Here are some essential steps:

- **Understand the Regulations:** Start by familiarizing yourself with the specific regulations that apply to your restaurant's location and operations. This includes the GDPR, PCI DSS, and local or industry-specific regulations.

- **Data Audit:** Conduct a thorough audit of the data your restaurant collects, processes, and stores. Document where it comes from, how it's used, and who can access it.

- **Consent Management:** When collecting customer data, including e-mail addresses, ensure you have explicit consent and provide clear information on how the data will be used. Implement procedures for customers to withdraw consent if they choose.

- **Security Measures:** Implement robust security measures to protect customer data, including encryption, access controls, and regular security assessments.

- **Data Protection Officer (DPO):** If you run a sizeable multi-location restaurant, consider appointing a Data Protection Officer or a responsible person within your organization to oversee data privacy compliance.

- **Employee Training:** Train your staff on data privacy best practices and the importance of compliance. Ensure they understand how to handle data securely.

- **Incident Response Plan:** As mentioned earlier, develop a comprehensive incident response plan that outlines the steps to take in case of a data breach, including notifying affected parties and authorities as required by law.

- **Third-Party Vendors:** If you use third-party vendors, such as POS system providers or reservation platforms, ensure they comply with relevant data privacy regulations.

- **Privacy Audits:** Conduct audits and assessments of your data privacy practices to identify and address any compliance gaps.

- **Legal Consultation:** Always seek legal counsel to ensure your compliance efforts align with the specific regulations affecting your restaurant.

Ensuring compliance with data privacy regulations is not just about avoiding legal troubles; it's about building and maintaining customer trust. Demonstrating your commitment to protecting their data will go a long way in fostering loyalty and enhancing your restaurant's reputation.

Key Takeaways

Social media marketing and online reviews have become integral components of restaurant success. Building a strong online presence and effectively engaging with your audience can significantly boost your restaurant's reputation and customer base.

Understanding the power of customer reviews and learning how to manage and respond to them gracefully is essential in today's digital landscape. Additionally, reputation management strategies can help you maintain a positive online presence, ensuring that your restaurant's image remains favorable to potential diners.

Additionally, ensuring data protection is critical to not only maintaining compliance but also to avoiding costly litigation and embarrassing public relations inquiries.

SECTION 4

Wrap-Up and Contact Information

In this section, we'll wrap up our journey together. I'll share some final thoughts, and provide my contact information. It has truly been a pleasure, and I appreciate sharing this journey with you.

CHAPTER 13
Final Thoughts and Contact Information

"Formal education will make you a living; self-education will make you a fortune."

Jim Rohn

I wanted to conclude this book with my favorite quote. It serves as a constant reminder that colleges, universities, and even the finest cooking schools can only provide a rudimentary foundation.

The real education comes in when you apply continuous self-directed learning, take risks, learn, and grow from your experiences. I sincerely hope you've enjoyed reading this book and that it has given you some practical ideas and strategies for eliminating costly table turnover mistakes and growing and scaling your restaurant.

I want you to feel excited, energized, and ready to apply what you've learned.

Stay in Touch

If you need anything, feel free to reach out at:

DonovanGarettMedia@gmail.com

Once again, thank you, and I look forward to hearing about your continued growth and success!

With Love and Gratitude

Donovan Garett

Also By Donovan Garett

Top Dollar Stylist Secrets: Amazing Strategies to Scale Your Barbershop / Beauty Salon to 7-Figures or More!

Learn the secrets that the world's top hair stylists use to turn their barbershops, hair salons, nail and brow art studios into incredible wealth-building machines! You'll learn strategies for properly marketing, advertising and promoting your business and your brand to others. This book is designed specifically with cosmetologists (barbers and hair stylists) in mind.

Amazon.com (Kindle): https://a.co/d/37r5rhp

Amazon.com (Paperback): https://a.co/d/gj2PNGS

The Ultimate Guide to Restaurant Marketing: In a Post-Covid Work From Home World

Today, small local independent restaurants are in crisis. They are completely assaulted on all sides by higher food costs, higher labor costs, an inflationary environment, lower attendance rates and a looming recession. The COVID-19 pandemic and the resulting work-from-home movement has had a major impact on consumer preferences, demands, and expectations of restaurants.

As a result, small restaurant owners must implement a solid marketing strategy and adapt it to reach remote workers and satisfy the needs, expectations and pain points of today's diners. To put it simply, yesterday's tactics don't work anymore. The days of simply hanging an "Open" sign outside your door are gone.

The *Ultimate Guide to Restaurant Marketing in a Post-Covid, Work-From-Home World* is not another watered-down operations manual. It will teach you exactly how to find and reach customers, communicate what makes your restaurant unique and make serious money even in recessions.

Amazon.com (Kindle): https://a.co/d/37r5rhp

Amazon.com (Paperback): https://a.co/d/gj2PNGS

www.ingramcontent.com/pod-product-compliance
Lightning Source LLC
Chambersburg PA
CBHW022055160426
43198CB00008B/237